MUSLIM CHRISTIAN DIALOGUE

Dr. H. M. Baagil, M. D.

Islamic Book Service

© All Right Reserved.

Muslim Christian Dialogue
Dr. H.M. Baagil, M.D.

ISBN: 81-7231-282-9

Reprint Edition: 2006

Published by *Abdul Naeem for*
Islamic Book Service
2872-74 Kucha Chelan, Darya Ganj, New Delhi-110002 (India)
Ph.: 23253514, 23286551, 23244556, Fax:011-23277913
E-mail: Islamic@eth.net, Ibsdelhi@del2.vsnl.net.in
Website:www.islamic-india.com

Our Associates:

Al Munna Book Shop Ltd.(Sharjah)
Fax:97165618723 E-mail: almunna@eim-ae
Branch:Dubai,Tel.: 04-352-9294

Azhar Academy Ltd.(London)
E-mail: sales@azharacademy.com
Website:www.azharacademy.com

Husami Book Depot
Machli Kaman, **Hyderabad**-500 002 **(A.P.)**
Tel.: 040-6680-6285

Printed in India

INTRODUCTION

In the Name of Allah, Most Gracious, Most Merciful.

I am grateful to Allah for having read the manuscript of Muslim-Christian Dialogue and being asked to write an introduction to this remarkably eye-opening book. Anyone interested in comparative religion will find in this book many surprises that challenge what many once believed to be absolute truth.

This work by Dr. Hasan M. Baagil reflects his meticulous and painstaking effort to present his findings clearly, concisely and thoroughly. As a result of his study of Christianity and the Bible over a four year period, Dr. Baagil, a dedicated Muslim, learned not only that Christians differ in their basic beliefs (Trinity, Divinity or Jesus, etc.), but also do not know that the Church doctrine contradicts with the Bible at numerous times and that the Bible even contradicts itself! His conversations with Christian clergy and laity during this period of study have provided the impetus for the Muslim-Christian Dialogue.

The reader will be surprised to learn that in the Bible, Jesus never claimed to be God; that Jesus did not die on the cross; that the miracles performed by Jesus were also performed by many other prophets, and even by disbelievers; and that Jesus himself prophesied the advent of the Prophet Muhammad, ﷺ. All of this and much more is detailed from the clear passages of the Bible. The question that obviously must be raised after witnessing such clear contradictions is: Is the Bible God's Word? The effort here by Dr. Baagil is not intended to deride Christian people and certainly not to mock Jesus and his teachings. Allah forbid! The intent is obviously to point out that false charges, misrepresentations and outright lies against Allah and His Prophets are in themselves deriding and mockery and a most odious thing.

Muslim-Christian Dialogue also makes clear the Islamic point of view in these matters and shows how the Qur'an, revealed to the Prophet Muhammad ﷺ some 600 years after the life of Jesus, corrects the errors that crept (knowingly or unknowingly) into the message that Jesus brought. This book should prove to be a very valuable asset to both Muslims and Christians, particularly given the interest in dialogue between the two faiths. God willing, this book will be an effective tool for Muslims in our efforts to invite Christians to Islam. Conversely, Christians should become more aware of what in fact the Bible says and what Jesus actually taught, as a result of studying this book. Indeed, as a Muslim the hope is that the non-Muslim will accept the Truth and bear witness to the Oneness of Allah and that Muhammad ﷺ is His slave servant and Messenger.

May Allah reward Dr. Baagil for his efforts to dispel the darkness. May Allah's peace be upon us all.

Muhammad A. Nubee

ACKNOWELDGEMENT

I am an American raised from childhood in Christian belief. Until I began my soul's quest for God, i.e. Allah, I had taken many matters of importance for granted.

After discussions and reading and rereading the manuscript of the present Muslim-Christian Dialogue, I have gone over the quotations from the King James Version of the Holy Bible and the Holy Qur'an.

I finally announce my *Shahadah* (Testimony) publicly in English than in Arabic: I bear witness that there is no deity except Allah, Who has no partner and Muhammad [ﷺ] is His servant and messenger, *(Ashhadu al-la Ilaha illal-lahu wahdahu la shareekalahu wa ashhadu anna Muhammadan abduhu wa rasuluhu).*

Through this very basic and simple testimony I believe many people will submit to Allah in spirit and truth.

I hope that this short and easy-to-read booklet will be read worldwide and will attract many who are searching for a true belief where their minds may find rest and satisfaction.

Roy Earl. Johnson

NOTE FROM THE AUTHOR

In the Name of Allah, Most Gracious, Most Merciful.

This booklet has been written as the result of dialogues I had with Christian clergy as well as laity. The discussions were polite, pleasant, friendly and constructive without the slightest intention of hurting the religious feeling of any Christian. It is provocative and a challenge to Christianity. It is indispensable for those looking for the truth and those studying comparative religion.

C.	:	Christian
M or m	:	Muslim
	:	Sallal-lahu Alaihi Wasallam (May Allah's peace and blessings on him)
(P.B.U.H)	:	Peace Be Upon Them

H. M. Baagil, M.D.
January, 1984

CONTENTS

Dialogue

		Page
1.	The First Contact Between a Christian and a Muslim	1
2.	The Holy Bible	15
3.	The Doctrine of the Trinity	25
4.	The Doctrine of the Divinity of Jesus Christ	32
5.	The Doctrine of the Divine Sonship of Jesus	40
6.	Was Jesus Crucified?	44
7.	The Doctrine of Atonement and Original Sin	50

Muhammad ﷺ In The Bible

1.	Both Ishmael and Isaac Were Blessed	53
2.	Criterion of the Prophet by Jeremiah	58
3.	Until Shiloh Come	58
4.	Baca Is Mecca	59
5.	The House of My Glory	60
6.	Chariot of Asses and Chariot of Camels	61
7.	The Prophet Like Unto Moses	62
8.	My Servant, Messenger and Elect	64
9.	King David Called Him "My Lord"	66
10.	Art Thou That Prophet?	67
11.	Baptizing With the Holy Ghost and With Fire	68
12.	The Least in the Kingdom of Heaven	68
13.	Blessed Are the Peacemakers	68
14.	Comforter	69
15.	Revelation to Prophet Muhammad ﷺ	72
16.	References	73

THE FIRST CONTACT BETWEEN A CHRISTIAN AND A MUSLIM

C. Why have there been in the last decade many discussions held between Christians and Muslims about their beliefs?

M. I think because we both have several things in common. We believe in the One Creator who had sent many Prophets and in Jesus as the Messiah as well as the Word of God which had been denied by the Jews.

Our Holy Qur'an mentions in *Surah 3:45:* "[Remember] when the angels said, "O Mary! Verily Allah gives you the glad tidings of a Word from Him, his name will be Messiah Jesus, the son of Mary, held in honour in this world and in the hereafter, and of those who are near to Allah...."

Dialogues have been held everywhere in Europe, Canada, the USA and Australia. Even the Vatican is not spared where discussions were held between Vatican theologians and Egyptian Muslim scholars in Rome in 1970 and in Cairo in 1974 and 1978. Also between Vatican theologians and Saudi Arabian Muslim scholars in Rome in 1974. Many times in Colombo, not to mention Muslims invited by many churches to present Islam.

C. If Christianity is nearly two thousand years old and Islam more than fourteen hundred years, why were these discussions not held centuries ago?

M. For the last three to four centuries many Asian and African countries dominated by Muslims were colonized by Britain, France, Holland, Belgium, Spain and Portugal. Many Christian mission colonists tried to convert as many Muslims as they could by whatever means they had, by giving them medical treatment, clothes, food, jobs to the poor, but only a few were converted. A small part of the elite were converted to Christianity because of their prejudice that Christianity brought them to their civilization and progress of knowledge. They had a wrong notion because this progress was attained after the separation of state and church in Europe.

After the Second World War many Muslims from Asian and African countries were emigrating as workers and professionals to the Western Hemisphere, which brought them more in contact with the Christians. Also students were active in introducing Islam.

C. Do you see other reasons why many dialogues were held nowadays even by their respective missions?

M. I think the gap between both is becoming smaller as each is more tolerant, although both are still competing in getting more converts. I still remember my Christian teacher who used to say, "Muhammad ﷺ the imposter, the dreamer, the epileptic." You now find fewer writers depicting Islam in such a manner.

We Muslims feel closer to the Christians than to the Jews and disbelievers, as the Qur'an prophesied in *Surah 5:82:* "Thou wilt find the most vehement of mankind in hostility to those who believe (to be) the Jews and the idolators. And thou wilt find the nearest of them in affection to those who believe (to be) those who say: Lo! We are Christians. This is because there are among them priests and monks (i.e. persons entirely devoted to the service of God, as were the Muslims), and because they are not proud." Some Christian denominations are making tremendous progress now by acknowledging for the first time in history that Muhammad ﷺ descended from Ishmael through his second son Kedar. The Davis Dictionary of the Bible, 1980, sponsored by the Board of Christian Education of the Presbyterian Church in the USA, writes under the word Kedar: "...A tribe descended from Ishmael *(Gen. 25:13)* ...The people of Kedar were Pliny's Cedrai, and from their tribe Muhammad ﷺ ultimately arose." The International Standard Bible Encyclopaedia quotes the following from A.S. Fulton: "...Of the Ishmaelite tribes, Kedar must have been one of the most important, and thus in later times the name came to be applied to all the wild tribes of the desert. It is through Kedar (Arabic Keidar) that Muslim genealogists trace the descent of Muhammad ﷺ from Ishmael."

Also Smith's Bible Dictionary will not stay behind and prints the following: "Kedar (black). Second son of Ishmael *(Gen. 25:13)* ...Muhammad ﷺ traces his lineage to Abraham through the celebrated Koreish tribe, which sprang from Kedar. The Arabs in the Hejaz are called Beni Harb (men of war), and are Ishmaelites as of old, from their beginning. Palgrave says their language is as pure now as when the Koran was written *(A.D. 610)*, having remained unchanged more than 1200 years; a fine proof of the permanency of Eastern Institutions."

The biggest asset brought by Muslim immigrants to the Western hemisphere is not their manpower but the Islam which is now taking root here. Many mosques and Islamic centers are established and many are reverted into Islam. I prefer the word reverted and not converted, as everybody is born in submission of Allah, i.e. Islam, this is the nature of every child born. The parents or the community convert him to Judaism, Christianity, other faiths, or atheism.

This is also a proof that Islam is not spreading by the sword but simply by propagation by individuals or groups of Muslims. We don't have special missions organized as in Christian missions.

The world population has increased 136% from 1934 through 1984, Christianity with 47% and Islam with 235%. See *The Plain Truth*, February 1984, in its 50 Year Anniversary issue, quoting from *The World Almanac and Book of Facts 1935* and *Reader's Digest Almanac and Year-book 1983*.

C. If all three religions, Judaism, Christianity and Islam, are claiming to emanate from the One and same Creator, why do they differ?

M. All Prophets from Adam to Muhammad ﷺ were sent with the same message: that is, the total submission of mankind to Allah. This submission in Arabic is called Islam; Islam also means Peace, peace between the Creator and His creatures. Unlike the names Judaism and Christianity, this name Islam has been given by Allah, the Creator Himself, as mentioned in *Surah 5:3*, "This day I have perfected your religion for you and completed My favour on you, and have chosen for you as the way of life al-Islam as your religion." Neither the name Judaism nor Christianity is found in the Bible, not even in a Bible dictionary. No Israelite prophet mentioned the word Judaism. Jesus never claimed to establish Christianity on earth and never called himself a Christian. The word Christian is mentioned only three times in the New Testament and first by pagans and Jews in Antioch about 43 A.D., long after Jesus had left this earth. Read in *Acts 11:26*, "...And the disciples were called Christians first in Antioch."

Later by King Agrippa II to Paul in *Acts 26:28*, "Then Agrippa said unto Paul, Almost thou persuadest me to be a Christian."

So the name Christian was first given by foes rather than friends. And finally by Peter in his letter to comfort the faithful in I *Peter 4:16*: "Yet if any man suffer as a Christian, let him not be ashamed..."

The first Muslim on earth is not Muhammad but Abraham who submitted totally to Allah. But Islam as a way of life had been revealed to other prophets prior to Abraham like Adam and Noah. Then Islam follows as the way of life for all humanity.

C. How could Abraham be a Muslim? He is known as a Jew!

M. A Jew? Who told you that?

C. We are taught that; it must be confirmed by the Bible, too.

M. Can you show me where in the Bible it says that he was a Jew? If you can't find it quickly, let me help you. Read *Genesis 11:31*.

C. "And Terah took Abram his son, and Lot the son of Haran his son's son, and Sarai his daughter-in-law, his son Abram's wife, and they went forth with them from Ur of the Chaldees, to go into the land of Canaan; and they came unto Haran and dwelt there."

C. So Abraham who was born in Ur of Chaldees could not have been a Jew. First because Ur of Chaldees was in Mesopotamia, which is now a part of Iraq. He was then more an Arab than a Jew. Secondly the name Jew came after the existence of Judah, the great-grandson of Abraham *(see chart on page 6)*. Read further, *Genesis 12:4 and 5*.

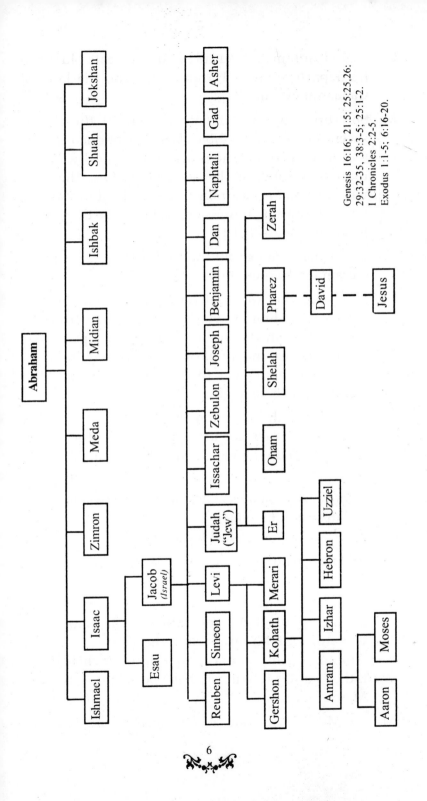

C. "...and Abram was seventy and five years old when he departed out of Haran... and into the land of Canaan they came."

M. So Abraham emigrated to Canaan at the age of seventy-five and the Bible clearly mentioned that he was there a stranger in Genesis 17:8, "And I will give unto thee, and to thy seed after thee, the land wherein thou art a stranger, all the land of Canaan, for an everlasting possession; and I will be their God." Read now Genesis 14:13.

C. "And there came one that had escaped, and told Abram the Hebrew;"

M. How can you call Abraham a Jew if the Bible itself calls him a Hebrew which means a man from the other side of the Euphrates. It also means pertaining to Eber, a descendant of Shem. Read now in Genesis 32:28 what happened to the name of Jacob after wrestling with an angel.

C. "And he said, Thy name shall be called no more Jacob, but Israel; for as a prince hast thou power with God and with men, and hast prevailed."

M. So Abraham was a Hebrew. The descendants of Jacob were Israelites consisting of the twelve tribes. Judah was nicknamed "Jew" so that only Judah's descendants were called Jews originally.

To know who Moses really was, read Exodus 6:16-20.

C. "And these are the names of the sons of Levi according to their generations; Ghershon, and Kohath, and Merari... And the sons of Kohath: Amram... And Amram took him Jochebed his father's sister to wife; and she bore him Aaron and Moses."

M. So Moses was not a Jew because he was not

descended from Judah but a Levite. Moses was the "law-giver" (Torah is law) to the children of Israel.

C. How can you explain that?

M. Because we are using the Holy Qur'an as standard. You can explain the Bible and correct the Jewish and Christian prejudice with the context of the Qur'an. It is the last revealed Book which has never been corrupted or adulterated. Its contents have been guaranteed by Allah in Surah 2:2: "This is the Scripture whereof there is no doubt..." and also in Surah 15:9, "No doubt We have sent down the Qur'an and surely We will guard it (from corruption)." This verse is a challenge to mankind. It is a clear fact that more than fourteen hundred years have passed and not a single word of this Qur'an has been changed although disbelievers tried their utmost to change it, but they failed miserably in their efforts. As it is mentioned in this Holy Verse: "We will guard this Book," by Allah, He has guarded it.

On the contrary, all the other holy books (Torah, Psalms, Gospels, etc.) have been adulterated in the form of additions, deletions or alterations from the original.

C. What does the Qur'an say about Abraham and Moses that you can deduce it from the Bible?

M. In Surah 3:65, "O people of the Scripture [Jews and Christians]! Why do you dispute about Abraham, while the Torah and the Gospel were not revealed till after him? Have you then no sense?"

And in Surah 3:67, "Abraham was neither a Jew nor a Christian, but he was a true Muslim (worshipper of none but Allah alone) and he joined none in worship with Allah."

In Surah 2:140, "Or say you that Abraham, Ishmael,

Isaac, Jacob and the twelve sons of Jacob were Jews or Christians? Say (O' Muhammad ﷺ), "Do you know better or does Allah (know better)? And who is more unjust than he who conceals the testimony he has from Allah? And Allah is not unaware of what you do." Of course they were not Jews or Christians as the name Jews came after Judah and the name Christians came long after Jesus had left.

C. It feels strange to hear the name Allah. Why don't you say God if you speak English?

M. Yes, indeed, the name of Allah seems to be strange to non-Muslims but this name has been used by all Prophets since Adam until Muhammad ﷺ. It is a contraction of the two Arabic words Al-Ilah, i.e. The God. By dropping the letter "I" you will find the word Allah. According to its position in an Arabic sentence it can have the form Allaha which is close to the Hebrew name of the Creator, i.e. Eloha. But the Jews are using wrongly the plural from Elohim which denotes more than one God. The word Allaha sounds closer to the Aramaic word for God used by Jesus, namely Alaha (see Encyclopedia Britannica 1980 under Allah and Elohim). So while the name Allah is strange to non-Muslims, it is not strange to all Prophets from Adam to Muhammad ﷺ, as they propagated in principle the same Islam, i.e. total submission, and the word Allah denotes the personal name of the Supreme Being. It is not subject to plurality or gender, so there is no such thing as Allahs, or male or female Allah, as there is Gods or God and Goddess. It is confusing to use the word God as many English-speaking Christians still consider Jesus as God. Even the word Creator is also confusing, as many Christians still maintain that

Jesus had created the world. Not only the name Allah is strange, but also the way Muslims worship Allah with ablution, bowing, kneeling, prostration and fasting is strange to non-Muslims, but not strange to all Prophets. While ablution (washing of face, arms, feet, and moistening of the hair) prior to worship is abandoned by modern Christians, it is still required by Muslims and previous Prophets, as seen in the following passages of the Bible: *Exodus 40:31-32:* "And Moses and Aaron and his sons washed their hands and their feet thereat; When they went into the tent of the congregation, and when they came near unto the altar, they washed; as the Lord commanded Moses." Although Paul made many changes in Jesus' teaching, he was still faithful in respect to ablution as seen in *Acts 21:26,* "Then Paul took the men, and the next day purifying himself with them entered into the temple..." Muslim women perform their prayer with their head covered as in I *Corinthians 11:5,6* and 13, "But every woman that prayeth or prophesieth with her head uncovered dishonoureth her head: for that is even all one as if she were shaven. For if the woman be not covered, let her also be shorn: but if it be a shame for a woman to be shorn or shaven, let her be covered... Judge in yourselves: is it comely that a woman pray unto God uncovered?" Muslims worship with bowing, kneeling, prostration and without shoes as done by previous Prophets: Psalm 95:6, "O come, let us worship and bow down: let us kneel before the Lord our maker." *Joshua 5:14,* "And Joshua fell on his face to the earth, and did worship... *I Kings 18:42,* "And Elijah went up to the top of Carmel; and he cast himself down upon the earth, and put his face between his knees." *Numbers 20:6,* "...and they [Moses and Aaron] fell upon their faces: and the glory of the Lord appeared upon them." *Genesis 17:3*, "And Abram fell on his face: and God talked with him, saying..." *Exodus 3:5* and *Acts 7:33*, "And he [God] said [to Moses], Draw not nigh hither: put off thy shoes from off thy feet, for the place whereon thou standest is holy ground."

A Christian will shiver in hearing that Pilgrimage or Haj as is now done by Muslims by circumambulating around the sacred stone Ka'bah in Mecca, had been performed by many Prophets, even by the Israelite Prophets.

C. I never read Pilgrimage or sacred stone in the Bible.

M. This has been mentioned clearly several times but overlooked by Bible readers:

1. Jacob on his way to Padan-aram saw a vision and built the next morning a pillar of stone which he called Beth-El, i.e. the House of the Lord *(Genesis 28:18-19)*.

2. Years later the same Prophet, Jacob, was ordered by Allah to go to Beth-El *(Genesis 25:4,14,15)*. Jacob removed all the strange Gods prior to going there. Later also Prophet Muhammad ﷺ removed all idols around the sacred stone Ka'bah in Mecca.

3. Another pillar was built by Jacob and his father-in-law Laban *(Genesis 31:45-49)*: "And Jacob took a stone, and set it up for a pillar. And Jacob said unto his brethren, Gather stones; and they took stones, and made a heap; and they did eat there upon the heap. And Laban called it Jegar-sahadutha, but Jacob called it Galeed... And Mizpah; for he said, The Lord watch between me and thee..."

4. Jephthah and Ammon had a war against each other. Jephthah swore to the Lord in Mizpeh of Gilead to sacrifice his only daughter if he won. He did win, and burnt his daughter there alive as an offering to the Lord *(Judges 11:29-39)*.

5. Four hundred thousand swordsmen from the eleven tribes of Israel swore before the Lord in Mizpeh to exterminate the tribes of Benjamin *(Judges 20 and 21)*.

6. The children of Israel under Samuel swore in Mizpeh to destroy their idols if they won against the Philistines *(I Samuel 7)*.

7. The whole nation of Israel assembled in Mizpeh when Samuel was appointed king of Israel *(I Samuel 10)*.

It is obvious now that there is no Mizpeh left in the world except the oldest one in the Holy City of Mecca built by Abraham and his son Ishmael, from whom later Prophet Muhammad ﷺ arose. Muslims are really the followers of all Prophets. I can tell you other things about Muslims, Islam and Muhammad ﷺ in the Bible, but why should you know this if you are not looking for the truth?

C. I am sure of my own belief as a Christian but I am stimulated to know more about both religions. I feel sometimes ridiculed as a Christian after reading books written by Muslims.

M. Did it affect you in your religious life?

C. Yes, I am not going to Church as regularly as before. I have been secretly reading books written by Muslims. I have asked several Muslims what was not clear to me, but not to my satisfaction. I am looking for a belief that I can rely on, that can give me peace of mind, scientifically acceptable, and not just believe in it blindly.

M. It should be like that. I appreciate your attitude. But we are not allowed to allure anyone. We propagate only to those who want to listen to us.

C. But I am free to choose any belief I like and nobody can stop me.

M. Yes, there is no compulsion in religion.

C. Why are Muslims calling other people to accept their belief, then?

M. As Christians ask the Jews to accept Jesus as the Messiah, we Muslims ask the Christians as well as Jews and all mankind to accept Muhammad ﷺ as the Seal of all Prophets. Our Prophet Muhammad ﷺ said: "Convey my message even one ayah (verse of the Holy Qur'an)."

Also, Isaiah mentioned in chapter 21:13, "The burden upon Arabia," which means the responsibility of the Muslim Arabs, of course of all Muslims now, to spread the Islam. Isaiah mentioned this after he saw in a vision a chariot of asses and a chariot of camels (21:7), "And he saw a chariot with a couple of horsemen, a chariot of asses, and a chariot of camels; and he hearkened diligently with much heed."

The chariot of asses turned out to be Jesus who entered Jerusalem (John 12:14; Matthew 21:5). Who then was the chariot of camels? It could not be other than Muhammad ﷺ who came about six hundred years after the advent of the Messiah. If this is not accepted, then this prophecy has not yet been fulfilled.

C. Your explanation stimulates me to review the Bible more carefully. I would like to get more discussions with you.

M. Yes, if you are successful in this world, it doesn't mean that you will be successful in the hereafter. The hereafter is much better and more lasting than this life. People are now becoming more materialistic and secular. Let us come together several times and discuss the differences frankly and without prejudice. Islam is based on reason, and you should not just accept it. Even your Bible says, "Prove all things; hold fast that which is good" *(I Thessalonians 5:21)*.

C. You quoted just now "chariot of camels" from Isaiah and made the conclusion that it was Muhammad ﷺ. Is he then prophesied in the Bible?

M. Sure.

C. In the Old or New Testament?

M. In both. But you cannot recognize him in the Bible as long as you don't believe in the Oneness of God. I mean as long as you still believe in the Trinity, the Divinity of Jesus, the Divine Sonship of Jesus, the Original Sin and the Atonement. All these are doctrines made by men. Jesus had prophesied *(Matthew 15:9)* that people will worship him uselessly and believing in doctrines made by men: "But in vain they do worship me, teaching for doctrines the commandments of men."

THE HOLY BIBLE

M. Are you sure that the Bible is holy?

C. Yes, I am very sure about it; it is God's Word.

M. Read what Luke said about his recording in 1:2 and 3.

C. "Even as they delivered them unto us, which from the beginning were eyewitnesses, and ministers of the word; It seemed good to me also, having had perfect understanding of all things from the very first, to write unto thee in order, most excellent Theophilus."

M. If Luke said that he himself was not an eyewitness and the knowledge he gathered was from eyewitnesses and not as words inspired by God, do you still believe the Bible is God's word?

C. Maybe only this part is not God's word.

M. History has shown that the Bible suffered changes throughout the ages. The Revised Standard Version 1952 and 1971, the New American Standard Bible and the New World Translation of the Holy Scriptures have expunged certain verses compared with the King James Version. Reader's Digest has reduced the Old Testament by fifty percent and the New Testament condensed by about twenty-five percent. Some years ago Christian theologians wanted to "desex" the Bible. Does "holy" mean that the Bible is free from error?

C. Yes, that is so. But what kind of error do you mean?

M. Suppose one verse states that a certain person died at the age of fifty years and another verse states that the same person died at the age of sixty years, can both statements be right?

C. No, both statements can never be right. Only one can be right or both are wrong.

M. If a holy book contains conflicting verses, do you still consider it holy?

C. Of course not, because a Holy Scripture is a revelation from God and it should be impossible to contain mistakes or conflicting verses.

M. Then it's not holy again.

C. Right; its holiness disappears.

M. If so, you can't trust it one hundred percent. What could be the causes then?

C. It could be a mistake in the recording; deliberate changes by scribes; deletion or addition.

M. If there are conflicting verses in the Bible, do you still consider it holy?

C. I don't believe that the Bible is not holy, since I don't see any conflicting verses in it.

M. There are many conflicting verses in it.

C. In the Old or New Testament?

M. In both Testaments. These are some of them:

II Samuel 8:4	I Chronicles 18:4
And David took from him a thousand chariots and *seven hundred* horsemen, and twenty thousand footmen...	And David took from him a thousand chariots and *seven thousand* horsemen, and twenty thousand footmen.

Q. Seven hundred or seven thousand?

II Samuel 8:9-10	I Chronicles 18:9-10
When *Toi* king of Hamath heard that David had smitten all the host of *Hadadezer*, Then *Toi* sent *Joram* his son unto king	Now when *Tou* king of Hamath heard how David had smitten all the host of *Hadarezer* king of Zobah; He sent *Hadoram* his son to king

David, to salute him, and to bless him, because he had fought against *Hadadezer*, and had smitten him; for *Hadadezer* had wars with *Toi*. And *Joram* with him vessels of silver, and vessels of gold, and vessels of brass.

David, to enquire of his welfare, and to congratulate him, because he had fought against *Hadarezer*, and smitten him; (for *Hadarezer* had war with *Tou*;) and with him all manner of vessels of gold and silver and brass.

Q. Toi or Tou, Joram or Hadoram, Hadadezer or Hadarezer?

II Samuel 10:18

And the Syrians fled before Israel; and David slew the men of *seven hundred chariots* of the Syrians, and *forty thousand horsemen*, and smote *shobach* the captain of their host, who died there.

I Chronicles 19:18

But the Syrians fled before Israel; and David slew of the Syrians *seven thousand men* which fought in chariots, and *forty thousand footmen* and killed *Shophach* the captain of the host.

Q. Seven hundred chariots or seven thousand men? Forty thousand horsemen or footmen? Shobach or Shophach?

II Kings 8:26

Two and twenty years old was Ahaziah when he began to reign:

II Chronicles 22:2

Forty and two years old was Ahaziah when he began to reign,

Q. Twenty-two or forty-two years?

II Kings 24:8

Jehoiachim was *eighteen years* old when he began to reign, and he reigned in Jerusalem *three months*.

II Chronicles 36:9

Jehoiachim was *eight years* old when he began to reign, and he reigned *three months and ten days* in Jerusalem.

Q. Eighteen years or eight years? Three months or three months and ten days?

II Samuel 23:8	I Chronicles 11:11
These be the names of the mighty men whom David had: The *Tachmonite* that sat in the seat, chief among the captains; the same was Adino the Eznite: he lift up his spear against *eight hundred*, whom he slew at one time.	And this is the number of the mighty men whom David had: Jashobeam, an *Hachmonite*, the chief of the captains; he lifted up his spear against *three hundred* slain by him at one time.

Q. Tachmonite or Hachmonite? Eight hundred or three hundred?

II Samuel 24:1	I Chronicles 21:1
And again the anger of the Lord was kindled against Israel, and he moved David against them to say, Go, number Israel and Judah.	And *Satan* stood up against Israel, and provoked David to number Israel.

Q. Is the Lord of David then Satan? God forbid!

II Samuel 6:23	II Samuel 21:8
Therefore Michal the daughter of Saul had *no child* until the day of her death.	But the king took the two sons of Rizpah the daughter of Aiah, whom she bare unto Saul, Armoni and Mephilbosheth; and *the five sons* of Michal the daughter of Saul, whom she brought up for Adriel the son of Barzilai the Meholathite.

Q. Did Michal have children or not? *Note:* The name Michal in *II Samuel 21:8* is still present in the King James version and the New World Translation of the Holy Scripture used by the Jehovah's Witnesses, but is changed to Merab in the New American Standard Bible 1973.

C. I never saw it before. Are there still many?

M. Do you want to know more? Is this not enough to deny its holiness? See *Genesis 6:3*, "And the Lord said, My spirit shall not always strive with man, for that he also is flesh: yet his days shall be an hundred and twenty years."

But how old was Noah when he died? More than a hundred and twenty years. See *Genesis 9:29*, "And all the days of Noah were nine hundred and fifty years when he died." Some Christian theologians maintain not that the maximum age of man will be a hundred and twenty years but that the flood would come in a hundred and twenty years. Even this doesn't fit because at the time of the flood Noah should have been six hundred and twenty (500 + 120) years old, but the Bible states six hundred years. Study these verses — *Genesis 5:32*, "And Noah was five hundred years old...;" *Genesis 7:6*, "And Noah was six hundred years old when the flood of waters was upon the earth."

Christianity believes that God created man in his image: white, black or any else, male or female? This is according to *Genesis 1:26*, "And God said, Let us make man in our image, after our likeness..." But this contradicts *Isaiah 40:18* and *25*, "To whom then will ye liken God? Or what likeness will ye compare unto him?... To whom then will ye liken me, or shall I be equal? saith the Holy One." See also *Psalm 89:6*,

"For who in the heaven can be compared unto the Lord? who among the sons of the mighty can be likened unto the Lord?" And *Jeremiah* 10:6,7, "Forasmuch as there is none like unto thee, O Lord... there is none like unto thee."

C. But all these are in the Old Testament.

M. Let's go to the New Testament now.

John 5:37	John 14:9
Ye have neither heard his [God's] voice at any time, nor seen his shape.	...he that hath seen me hath seen the Father...

John 5:31	John 8:14
If I bear witness of myself, *my witness is not true*.	Jesus answered and said unto them, Though I bear record of myself, *yet my record is true*.

These are only some of the contradictions in the New Testament. You will find more if we discuss together the truth of the doctrines of modern Christianity like the Trinity, Divinity of Jesus Christ, Divine Sonship of Jesus, Original Sin and Atonement, not to mention the degrading of many Prophets in the Bible as worshippers of false gods and accusing them of incest, rape and adultery.

C. Where do you find that in the Bible?

M. Noah is shown to have been drunk to the point of becoming naked in the presence of his grown-up sons (Genesis 9:23-24): "And Shem and Japhet took a garment, and laid it upon both their shoulders, and went backward and covered the nakedness of their father; and their faces were backward, and they saw not their father's nakedness. And Noah awoke from his wine, and knew what his younger son had done unto him."

Solomon was accused not only of having a large harem but also of worshipping their false gods (I Kings 11:9-10): "And the Lord was angry with Solomon... And had commanded him concerning this thing, that he should not go after other gods: but he kept not that which the Lord commanded."

Aaron, as a Prophet who had accompanied his brother Moses to go to Pharaoh, was accused of having fashioned the golden calf for the Israelites to worship (Exodus 32:4): "And he [Aaron] received them [golden earrings] at their hand, and fashioned it with a graving tool, after he had made it a golden calf: and they said, These be thy gods, O Israel, which brought thee up out of the land of Egypt."

You will read of the incest of Prophet Lot with his two daughters (Genesis 19:36): "Thus were both the daughters of Lot with child by their father."

You will read of a Prophet who was married to two sisters at the same time (Genesis 29:28): "And Jacob did so, and fulfilled her week: and he [Laban] gave him Rachel his daughter to wife also."

And another Prophet accused of adultery *(II Samuel 11:4-5)*: "And David sent messengers, and took her [the wife of Uriah]; and she came in unto him, and he lay with her; for she was purified from her uncleanness; and she returned unto her house. And the woman conceived, and sent and told David, and said, I am with child."

My question is: How could David then be accepted in the genealogy of Jesus when it started with a person who committed adultery? Allah forbid it! Is this not in contradiction with what is mentioned in Deuteronomy 23:2, "A bastard shall not enter into the congregation of the Lord; even to his tenth generation shall he not enter into the congregation of the Lord."

Another allegation of incest along with rape by Ammon the son of David on his half-sister Tamar *(II Samuel 13:14)*: "Howbeit he [Ammon] would not hearken unto her voice: but being stronger than she [Tamar], forced her, and lay with her."

Still another multiple rape, by Absalom on David's concubines, was told in *II Samuel 16:33*, "So they spread Absalom a tent upon the top of the house, and Absalom went in unto his father's concubines in the sight of all Israel." (I can't believe that anybody in the world could do this, not even the barbarian.)

Another incest, by Judah and Tamar his daughter-in-law: Judah on his way to Timnath to shear his sheep saw Tamar; he thought her to be a harlot because she had her face covered *(Genesis 38:18)*: "...And he [Judah] gave it [signet, bracelet and staff] her, and came in unto her and she conceived by him."

Although Jews and Muslims are archenemies, no Muslim would dare to write a book and stamp any Israelite Prophet like Judah, David, Jesus, etc. (Allah's blessings and peace be upon all of them forever and ever) with rape, adultery, incest or prostitution.

All Prophets were sent by Allah for the guidance of mankind. Do you think that God had sent the wrong people for guidance?

C. I don't think so. But don't you believe in the Bible?

M. We believe in all Divine Scriptures, but in their original form. God sent to each nation a Prophet as a warner, and some of them with a Scripture as a guidance for that particular nation only. The Suhuf to Abraham, the Torah (part of the Old Testament) to Moses, the Zabur (Psalms) to David, and the Injeel (New Testament) to Jesus. None of the these Scriptures remain in their original form now. As part of Allah's original plan, He finally sent Muhammad ﷺ as the Seal of all Prophets with the Holy Qur'an as a guidance for all mankind, anywhere and anytime.

Jesus himself said that he was sent only to the people of Israel *(Matthew 15:24)*: "I am not sent but unto the lost sheep of the house of Israel." Also *(Matthew 1:21)*: "And she shall bring forth a son, and thou shalt call his name Jesus; for he shall save his people from their sins." He even said that he came not to make changes but to fulfil *(Matthew 5:17-18)*: "Think not that I am come to destroy the law, or the prophets: I am not come to destroy, but to fulfil. For verily I say unto you, Till heaven and earth pass, one jot or one tittle shall in no wise pass from the law, till all be fulfilled."

C. But in Mark 16:15, Jesus said, "Go ye into all the world, and preach the gospel to every creature."

M. This contradicts what is mentioned above in *Matthew 15:24* and *Matthew 1:21*. Secondly, *Mark 16:9-20* has been expunged in many Bibles. The New American Standard Bible put this part in brackets and wrote the following commentary: "Some of the oldest mss. Omit from verse 9 through 20." The New World Translation of the Holy Scriptures used by the Jehovah's Witnesses admits that certain ancient manuscripts add a long conclusion or a short conclusion after Mark 16:8 but some omit. And the Revised Standard version prints the following footnote: "Some of the most ancient authorities bring the book to a close at the end of verse 8..." This means also that the resurrection is not true as this is described in *Mark 16:9*.

C. But Jesus said in *Matthew 28:19:* "Go ye therefore, and teach all nations..."

M. "All nations" must be explained as all the twelve tribes of Israel; otherwise it contradicts *Matthew 15:24* and *Matthew 1:21*. In the New American Standard Bible and the New World Translation of the Holy Scriptures it is not translated as "all nations" but as "all the nations," which means the twelve tribes of Israel.

What do you think of the Bible now?

C. My belief in it starts to shake now.

M. I am sure you will be convinced of the authenticity of Islam after we have discussed our differences.

THE DOCTRINE OF THE TRINITY

M. Do you still believe in the Trinity?

C. Sure; it is written in the First Epistle of John (5:7 and 8): "For there are three that bear record in heaven, the Father, the Word, and the Holy Ghost: and these three are one. And there are three that bear witness in earth, the spirit, and the water, and the blood: and these three agree in one."

M. Oh, that is in the King James Version, authorized in 1611, and formed the strongest evidence for the Doctrine of the Trinity. But now this part, "the Father, the Word, and the Holy Ghost: and these three are one," has been expunged in the Revised Standard Version of 1952 and 1971 and in many other Bibles, as it was a gloss that had encroached on the Greek text.

I John 5:7 and 8 in the New American Standard Bible reads as follows: "And it is the Spirit who bears witness, because the Spirit is truth. For there are three that bear witness, the Spirit and the water and the blood, and the three are in agreement." Also, in the New World Translation of the Holy Scriptures used by the Jehovah's Witnesses, you will find: "For there are three witness bearers, the spirit and the water and the blood, and the three are in agreement." I can understand if you don't know that this important part has been removed, but I wonder why many ministers and preachers are not aware of this.

The Trinity is not Biblical. The word Trinity is not

even in the Bible or Bible dictionaries, was never taught by Jesus and was never mentioned by him. There is no basis or proof in the Bible whatsoever for the acceptance of the Trinity.

C. But in Matthew 28:19 we still find: "...baptizing them in the name of the Father, and of the Son, and of the Holy Spirit." This part is not removed yet; is this not a proof of the Trinity?

M. No. If you mention three persons are sitting or eating together, does it mean that they are forming one person? No. The formulation of the Trinity by Athanasius, an Egyptian deacon from Alexandria, was accepted by the Council of Nicaea in A.D. 325, i.e. more than three centuries after Jesus had left. No doubt Roman paganism had influence in this doctrine, the triune god; Sabbath was shifted to Sunday; December 25, which was the birthday of their sun-god Mithra, was introduced as Jesus' birthday, although the Bible clearly predicted and forbade the decoration of Christmas trees in *Jeremiah 10:2-5*, "Thus saith the Lord, Learn not the way of the heathen, and be not dismayed at the signs of heaven; for the heathen are dismayed at them. For the customs of the people are vain: for one cutteth a tree out of the forest, the work of the hands of the workman, with the axe. They deck it with silver and with gold, they fasten it with nails and with hammers, that it move not. They are upright as the palm tree, but speak not: they must needs be borne, because they cannot go. Be not afraid of them; for they cannot do evil, neither also is it in them to do good." Because Christianity and deviated a long way from the original teachings of Jesus, Allah then sent as part of His original plan His last Prophet, Muhammad ﷺ, as revivalist to restore all these changes: the Roman Julian calendar introduced as the Christian era; pork not prohibited; circumcision abolished by Paul *(Galatians 5:2)*: "Behold, I Paul say unto you, that if ye be circumcised, Christ shall profit you nothing."

The Holy Qur'an warns in *Surah 5:73:* "Surely they are disbelievers, those who said: Allah is one of the three in a Trinity.' But there is none who has the right to be worshiped but one God (i.e. Allah). And if they cease not from what they say, verily a painful torment will befall the disbelievers among them."

Do you still believe in the Trinity which was never taught by Jesus?

C. But God and Jesus are one *(John 14:11)*: "Believe me that I am in the Father, and the Father in me."

M. Read then *John 17:21.*

C. "That they [the disciples] all may be one; as thou, Father, are in me, and I in thee, that they may also be one in us..."

M. It is clear here that God and Jesus are one, but also that the disciples are one in Jesus and God. If Jesus is God because he is in God, why are the disciples then not God, as they all are like Jesus also in God? If God, Jesus and the Holy Ghost form one unit of Trinity, then with the disciples included they should form a God unit of fifteen.

C. But Jesus is God according to *John 14:9,* "...he that hath seen me hath seen the Father."

M. See to the context now — what is before and after this: *(John 14:8)*: "Philip saith unto him, Lord, shew us the Father, and it sufficeth us." *(John 14:9)*: "Jesus saith unto him, have I been so long time with you, and yet hast thou not known me, Philip? he that hath seen me hast seen the Father; and how sayest thou then, Shew us the Father?"

So finally Jesus asked Philip how to show the appearance of God of the disciples, which is not possible. You should believe in God by admiring His creation: the sun, the moon, all creation, and Jesus himself who was created by God. He said *(John 4:24)*: "God is a Spirit..." and *(John 5:37)*: "...ye have neither heard his voice at any time, nor seen his shape." How can you see a spirit then? What they saw was Jesus and not God. Also Paul said *(I Timothy 6:16)*: "...whom no man hath seen, nor can see..." So what you can see is never God.

Our Holy Qur'an says *(Surah 6:103)*: "Vision comprehendeth Him not, but He comprehendeth (all) vision. He is the Subtile, the Aware."

C. To be honest, it is difficult to deny what has been taught to us since childhood.

M. Maybe the following questions will give you a better understanding of the Trinity: What is the Holy Spirit?

C. The Holy Spirit is the Holy Ghost, is also God. We are taught, the Father is God, the Son is God, the Holy Ghost is God. We are not allowed to say Three Gods, but One God.

M. Read *Matthew 1:18*.

C. "Now the birth of Jesus Christ was on this wise: When as his mother Mary was espoused to Joseph, before they came together, she was found with child of the Holy Ghost."

M. Compare now with Luke 1:26 and 27.

C. "And in the sixth month the angel Gabriel was sent from God unto a city of Galilee, named Nazareth, To a virgin espoused to a man whose name was Joseph, of the house of David; and the virgin's name was Mary."

M. So in the miraculous birth of Jesus, Matthew mentioned the Holy Ghost and Luke mentioned the angel Gabriel. What is the Holy Ghost then?

C. The Holy Ghost is then the angel Gabriel.

M. Do you still believe in the Trinity now?

C. Then God is God, the Holy Ghost or the Holy Spirit is the angel Gabriel, and Jesus is...

M. Let me help you: Jesus is a Prophet, son of Mary.

C. How can you solve what we call a mystery?

M. We use the Holy Qur'an as the standard to correct changes made by men in the previously revealed scriptures. If you can now believe in One God, and Jesus, son of Mary, as a Prophet, why don't you go one step further and accept Muhammad ﷺ as the Last Mesenger? Read with me the Shahadah or Witness (Testimony), first in English, then in Arabic.

C. I bear witness that there is no deity except Allah, Who has no partner, and Muhammad ﷺ is His slave servant and messenger. Ash-hadu an-la Ilaha Illal-Lahu wahdahu la shareekalahu wa ash-hadu anna Muhammadan abduhu wa rasuluh.

But what about my great-grandparents? I would like to stay with them; they were all Christians.

M. Abraham had left his parents and great-grandparents when the Truth. i.e. Islam, was revealed to him. Everyone is responsible for himself. Maybe the Truth hadn't come to your ancestors as clearly as it comes to you now. The Holy Qur'an says in *Surah 17:15*, "Whoever goes right, then, he goes right only for his own soul's benefit. And whoever goes astray, then he goes astray only to his own loss. No laden soul can bear another's load. And We never punish until We have sent an apostle (to give warnings)."

So the Truth has come to you now and it is up to you.

C. Is it not possible to accept both Islam and Christianity?

M. There is no compulsion in religion. You can do whatever you want. But if you combine both faiths, you haven't surrendered to Allah yet. You are still a disbeliever, as He states in *Surah* 4:150-152: "Verily those who disbelieve in Allah and His messengers and wish to make distinction between Allah and His messengers [by believing in Allah and disbelieving in His messengers] saying 'We believe in some and reject others,' and wish to take a way in between [this and] that: They are disbelievers in truth. And We have prepared for disbelievers a humiliating torment. To those who believe in Allah and His messengers and make no distinction between any of them [messengers], We shall give them their rewards, and Allah is ever Oft-Forgiving, Most Merciful."

You may later agree with me if we discuss further.

C. Is it not better that we do not make any Confession or Shahadah, so that we are not committed?

M. As soon as you reach adulthood and you are mentally competent, you are then committed whether you make the Shahadah or not. Allah created this world not for nothing. He has supplied you with the organs to differentiate between right and wrong. He has sent many Prophets as warners. We are created to worship Him and that we may compete with each other in good deeds in this world.

Surah 3:191, "...Our Lord! You have not created [all] this without purpose, Glory to You!.."

Surah 90:8-10, "Have We not made for him [mankind] a pair of eyes? And a tongue and a pair of lips? And shown him the two ways [good and evil]?"

Surah 51:56, "And I created not the Jinns and mankind except they should worship Me [alone]." Every deed for the pleasure of Allah is worship.

Surah 18:7, "Verily! We have made that which is on earth as an adoration for it [the earth] in order that We may test them [mankind] as to which of them is better in deeds."

THE DOCTRINE OF THE DIVINITY OF JESUS CHRIST

M. Is Jesus God?

C. Yes. In the Gospel according to *John (1:1)*: "In the beginning was the Word, and the Word was with God, and the Word was God."

M. We have agreed that a Holy Scripture should not contain contradictions. If there are two conflicting verses, then only one can be true; both can never be true or both are wrong.

Jesus is then God according to John 1:1. Then how many Gods are there? Two at least. This then is in contradiction with many passages in the Bible: *(Deuteronomy 4:39)*: "...that the Lord he is God in heaven above, and upon the earth beneath: there is none else"; *(Deuteronomy 6:4)*: "Hear, O Israel: The Lord our God is one Lord"; *(Isaiah 43:10-11)*: "...that ye may know and believe me, and understand that I am he: before me there was no God formed, neither shall there be after me. I, even I, am the Lord; and beside me there is no saviour"; *(Isaiah 44:6)*: "Thus saith the Lord... I am the first, and I am the last; and beside me there is no God"; *(Isaiah 45:18)*: "For thus saith the Lord that created the heavens; God himself that formed the earth and made it; he hath established it, he created it not in vain, he formed it to-be inhabited: I am the Lord; and there is none else."

From *Isaiah 45:18* alone we can conclude that God alone was the Creator and no one else, not even Jesus, participated in the creation.

See further: *Deuteronomy 4:35; Exodus 8:10; II Samuel 7:22; I*

Kings 8:23; I Chronicles 17:20; Psalms 86:8, 89:6 and 113:5; Hosea 13:4; Zechariah 14:9.

C. But these are all in the Old Testament. Do you find it in the New Testament?

M. Sure. Read in *Mark 12:29* what Jesus himself said: "And Jesus answered him, The first of all the commandments is, Hear, O Israel: The Lord our God is one Lord."

(I *Cornithians 8:4*): "...we know that an idol is nothing in the world, and that there is none other God but one." (I *Timothy 2:5*): "For there is one God, and one mediator between God and men, the man Christ Jesus." Look to the expression "the man Christ Jesus." Now you can either say that John 1:1 is right and all these other verses are wrong, or the reverse.

C. Difficult to judge!

M. Let us see it from the Qur'anic point of view, and this corresponds with what Jesus himself said in the Bible. Jesus is mentioned several times in the Qur'an as a Word from Allah. In *Surah 3:39*, "Then the angels called to him [Zechariah] while he was standing in prayer in the chamber (saying): Allah gives you glad tidings of John [i.e. the Baptist] believing in a Word from Allah [i.e. Jesus, son of Mary], noble, keeping away from sexual relations with women, a prophet, and one of the righteous."

In the same *Surah 3*, again mentioned in *verse 45*, "[Remember] when the angels said: "O Mary! Verily Allah gives you the glad tidings of a Word from Him, his name will be Messiah Jesus, the son of Mary, held in honour in this world and the Hereafter, and of those who are near to Allah." In both verses of the Holy Qur'an, Jesus is also called a Word from Allah, i.e. a Word coming from Allah or belonging to Allah, in correspondence with *I Corinthians 3:23*, "And ye are Christ's; and Christ is God's. "*John 1:1* should also have been written: "...and the Word was God's." The mistake could have been in the translation from Aramaic to Greek, deliberately or not. In the Greek language Theos is God, but Theou means God's *(see Greek dictionary, Greek Bible, or Muhammad ﷺ in the Bible by Prof. Abdul-Ahad Dawud, former Bishop of Uramiah, page 16)*. A difference of only one letter but big consequences.

C. Why is Jesus called the Word of God in both Scriptures?

M. The creation of Jesus in the womb of Mary was without the agency of a sperm, just only with the decree of Allah, "Be," as mentioned in the same *Surah 3:47*, "She [Mary] said; 'O, my Lord! How shall I have a son when no man has touched me?' He said: 'So [it will be], for Allah creates what He will. When He has decreed something, He says to it only "Be" and it is."

C. Jesus is God because he is filled with the Holy Spirit.

M. Why don't you consider other people divine who are also filled with the Holy Ghost? *(Acts 11:24)*: "For he [Barnabas] was a good man, and full of the Holy Ghost and of faith; and much people was added unto the Lord." *(Acts 5:32)*: "And we are his witnesses of these things; and so is also the Holy Ghost, whom God hath given to them that obey him."

See further *Acts 6:5; II Peter 1:21; II Timothy 1:14; I Corinthians 2:16; Luke 1:41*.

C. But Jesus was filled with the Holy Ghost while he was still in his mother's womb.

M. The same was true with John the Baptist *(Luke 1:13, 15)*: "But the angel said unto him, Fear not,

Zacharias: for thy prayer is heard; and thy wife Elizabeth shall bear thee a son, and thou shalt call his name John. For he shall be great in the sight of the lord, and he shall be filled with the Holy Ghost, even from his mother's womb."

C. But Jesus could do mircacles. He fed five thousand people with only five loaves and two fishes.

M. The same was done by Elisha and Elijah. Elisha fed a hundred people with twenty barley loaves and a few ears of corn *(II Kings 4:44)*: "So he set it before them, and they did eat, and left thereof, according to the word of the Lord." Elisha secured the increase of a widow's oil and he said to her *(II Kings 4:7)*: "Go, sell the oil, and pay thy debt, and live thou and thy children of the rest." See also *I Kings 17:16*, "And the barrel of meal wasted not, neither did the cruse of oil fail, according to the word of the Lord, which he spake by Elijah." Also *I Kings 17:6*, "And the ravens brought him [Elijah] bread and flesh in the morning, bread and flesh in the evening; and he drank of the brook."

C. But Jesus could heal leprosy.

M. Also Elisha told Naaman who was a leper to wash in the Jordan river *(II Kings 5:14)*: "Then went he [Naaman] down, and dipped himself seven times in Jordan, according to the saying of the man of God [Elisha]: and his flesh came again like unto a flesh of a little child, and he was clean."

C. But Jesus could cause a blind man to see again.

M. Also Elisha did *(II Kings 6:17)*: "And Elisha prayed, and said, Lord, I pray thee, open his eyes, that he may see. And the Lord opened the eyes of the young man: and he saw..." *(II Kings 6:20)*: "And it came to pass, when they were come into Samaria, that Elisha said, Lord open the eyes of these men, that they may see. And the Lord opened their eyes, and they saw; and behold, they were in the midst of Samaria."

Elisha was also told to cause blindness *(II Kings 6:18)*: "And when they came down to him, Elisha prayed unto the Lord, and said, Smite this people, I pray thee, with blindness. And he smote them with blindness according to the word of Elisha."

C. Jesus, could raise the dead.

M. Compare with Elijah *(I Kings 17:22)*: "And the Lord heard the voice of Elijah: and the soul of the child came into him again, and he revived." Compare also with Elisha *(II Kings 4:34)*: "And the [Elisha] went up, and lay upon the child, and put his mouth upon his mouth, and his eyes upon his eyes, and his hands upon his hands; and he stretched himself upon the child; and the flesh of the child waxed warm."

Even the dead bones of Elisha could restore a dead body to life by touching only *(II Kings 13:21)*: "And it came to pass, as they were burying a man, that, behold, they spied a band of men; and they cast the man into the sepulchre of Elisha: and when the man was let down, and touched the bones of Elisha, he revived, and stood up on his feet."

C. But Jesus walked upon the water.

M. Moses stretched out his arms over the sea *(Exodus 14:22)*: "And the children of Israel went into the midst of the sea upon the dry ground; and the waters were a wall unto them on their right hand, and on their left."

C. But Jesus could cast out devils.

M. Jesus himself admitted that other people could do it *(Matthew 12:27* and *Luke 11:19)*: "And if I by Beelzebub cast out devils, by whom do your children cast them out? therefore shall they be your judges."

Also the disciples could cast out devils as Jesus said *(Matthew 7:22)*: "Many will say to me in that day, Lord, have we not prophesied in thy name: and in thy name have cast out devils? and in thy name done many wonderful works?"

Even false prophets would do wonders, as prophesied by Jesus himself *(Matthew 24:24)*: "For there shall arise false Christs, and false prophets, and shall shew great signs and wonders; insomuch that, if it were possible, they shall deceive the very elect."

C. But Elijah and Elisha did wonder through praying to the Lord.

M. Jesus also did the miracles with the grace of God, as he himself said *(John 5:30)*: "I can of mine own self do nothing..." and *(Luke 11:20)*: "But if I with the finger of God cast out devils, no doubt the Kingdom of God is come upon you."

All miracles performed by Jesus had been done by previous prophets, disciples, and even unbelievers. On the other hand, Jesus could do no mighty work where there was unbelief *(Mark 6:5,6)*: "And he could there do no mighty work, save that he laid his hands upon a few sick folk, and healed them. And he marvelled because of their unbelief. And he went around about the villages, teaching."

C. But Jesus was resurrected three days after he died.

M. We will talk later about his crucifixion because there are so many controversies about it. I'll only say now briefly that it was a gospel of Paul, who never saw Jesus alive *(II Timothy 2:8)*: "Remember that Jesus Christ of the seed of David was raised from the dead according to my gospel."

The gospel of resurrection in *Mark 16:9-20* has also been removed in many Bibles. If not removed it is printed in small print or between two brackets and with commentary. See Revised Standard Version, New American Standard Bible and New World Translation of the Holy Scriptures of the Jehovah's Witnesses. Let me ask you one thing: did Jesus ever claim to be God or to say, "Here am I, your God, and worship me"?

C. No, but he is God and man.

M. But did he ever claim that?

C. No.

M. Indeed he had prophesied that people will worship him uselessly and will believe in doctrines not made by God but by men *(Matthew 15:9)*: "But in vain they do worship me, teaching for doctrines the commandments of men."

All doctrines of modern Christianity are made by men: the Trinity, Divine Sonship of Jesus, Divinity of Jesus Christ, Original Sin and Atonement. From Jesus' own sayings, recorded in the New Testament, it is clear that he never claimed divinity or identity to God: "I do nothing of myself" *(John 8:28)*; "My Father is greater than I" *(John 14:28)*; "The Lord our God is one Lord" *(Mark 12:29)*; "My God, my God, why hast thou forsaken me?" *(Mark 15:34)*; "Father, into thy hands I commend my spirit" *(Luke 23:46)*.

"But of that day and that hour knoweth no man, no, not the angels which are in heaven, neither the Son, but the Father" *(Mark 13:32)*. Jesus was called prophet, teacher from God, His servant, Messiah, and later was escalated to Son of God, and then God Himself.

Let us now use our reason: how can God be born by a mortal one as any other mortal?

Jesus slept while God never sleeps *(Psalm 121:4)*: "Behold, he that keepeth Israel shall neither slumber nor sleep." God should be powerful but how could people spit on him, crucify him as alleged. How could Jesus be God if he worshipped God as any other mortal *(Luke 5:16)*: "And he withdrew himself into the wilderness, and prayed."

Jesus was tempted by Satan for forty days *(Luke 4:1-13)* but in *James 1:13* is said: "...for God cannot be tempted with evil..." How can Jesus be God, then? We can rationalize further and further.

C. Yes, I myself can't understand it but we have to accept it blindly.

M. Is it not contradicting the Bible itself which says that you have to prove it *(I Thessalonians 5:21)*: "Prove all things; hold fast that which is good."

C. It's really confusing.

M. But *I Corinthians 14:33* says, "For God is not the author of confusion but of peace, as in all churches of the saints."

Doctrines made by men create confusion.

THE DOCTRINE OF THE DIVINE SONSHIP OF JESUS

M. Is Jesus Son of God?

C. Yes. Read in Matthew 3:17, when Jesus was baptized by John: "And lo a voice from heaven, saying, This is my beloved Son, in whom I am well pleased."

M. You should not accept the word Son literally, because many Prophets and we people are called in the Bible also, sons and children of God. Read Exodus 4:22.

C. "And thou [Moses] shalt say unto Pharaoh, Thus saith the Lord, Israel is my son, even my firstborn."

M. Here is Jacob (Israel) His firstborn son. *Read now II Samuel 7:13-14* or *I Chronicles 22:10.*

C. "He [Solomon] shall build a house for my name, and I will establish the throne of his kingdom for ever. I will be his father and he shall be my son..."

M. It will be confusing if you read *Jeremiah 31:9,* "I am a father to Israel and Ephraim is my firstborn." In *Exodus 4:22* just now, Israel was called firstborn, too. Who is now the real firstborn? Israel or Ephraim? Common people can be children of God; read Deuteronomy 14:1.

C. "Ye are the children of the Lord your God."

M. Common people can also be called firstborn, read *Romans 8:29.*

C. "For whom he did foreknow, he also did predestinate to be conformed to the image of his

Son, that he might be the firstborn of many brethren."

M. If all are firstborn, what is Jesus then?

C. He is the only begotten Son of God.

M. Long before Jesus was born, God said to David *(Psalm 2.7)*: "I will declare the decree: the Lord hath said unto me [David], Thou art my Son; this day have I begotten thee." So David is also God's begotten Son. The meaning of Son of God is not literal but metaphorical. It can be any one who is beloved by God. Jesus also said that God is not only his Father but also your Father *(Matthew 5:45, 48)*.

C. "That ye may be the children of your Father"; and "Be ye therefore perfect, even as your Father which is in heaven is perfect."

M. So you will see in many passages in the Bible "Son of God" which signifies love and affection, nearness to God, not applied to Jesus alone. You will see sons and daughters of God *(11 Corinthians 6:18)*: "And will be a Father unto you, and ye shall be my sons and daughters, saith the Lord Almighty." In view of these and other passages in the Bible, there is no reason whatsoever why Jesus should be regarded as Son of God in a literal or unique sense.

C. But he has no father; that is why he is Son of God.

M. Why do you consider Adam then not as Son of God. He lacked both father and mother, and is also called Son of God in *Luke 3:38*, "...Seth, which was the son of Adam, which was the son of God." Read *Hebrews 7:3*.

C. "Without father, without mother, without descent, having neither beginning of days, nor end of life; but made like unto the Son of God; abideth a priest continually."

M. Who is he? The answer is in *Hebrews 7:1:* "Melchisedec, king of Salem, priest of the most high God, who met Abraham..." He is more unique than Jesus or Adam. Why is he not preferred to be son of God or God himself?

C. What do you call Jesus then?

M. We Muslims call him Jesus, the son of Mary.

C. No one will deny this.

M. Yes, it is simple and nobody can deny it. Jesus called himself Son of man and refused to be called Son of God. *Read Luke 4:41.*

C. "And devils also came out of many, crying out, and saying, Thou art Christ the Son of God. And he rebuking them suffered them not to speak: for they knew that he was Christ."

M. It is clear here that he refused to be called Son of God. He refused again in *Luke 9:20* and *21*, and charged them too.

C. "He [Jesus] said unto them [the disciples], But whom say ye that I am? Peter answering said, The Christ of God. And he straightly charged them, and commanded them to tell no man that thing."

M. Jesus who was the expected Messiah, a Prophet, was escalated from teacher to Son of God, Lord, and finally God Himself. Read *John 3:2*, "The same came to Jesus by night, and said unto him, Rabbi, we know that thou art a teacher come from God..."; *(John 6:14):* "Then those men, when they had seen the miracle that Jesus did said, This is of a truth that prophet that should come into the world." Jesus is also called prophet in *John 7:40, Matthew 21:11, Luke 7:16* and *24:19. (Acts 9:20):* "And straightway he [Paul] preached Christ in the synagogues, that he is the Son of God." (You can conclude from here also that early Christians were still using synagogues, but later when Christianity deviated from the original teaching of Jesus, churches were established. Paul, Barnabas and the gentiles were expelled from the synagogues, as they were accused of blasphemy and pollution. See *Acts 13:50, 17:18* and *21:28.*) *Luke 2:11,* "For unto you is born this day in the city of David a Saviour, which is Christ the Lord." *John 1:1,* "In the beginning was the Word, and the Word was with God, and the Word was God."

WAS JESUS CRUCIFIED?

M. The Holy Qur'an states in *Surah* 4:157 that Jesus was not crucified: "And their [Jews'] boasting: 'We killed Messiah Jesus, son of Mary, the Apostle of Allah,' but they [Jews] killed him not, nor crucified him..." Do you still believe that he died on the cross?

C. Yes, he died and was then resurrected.

M. We all agree that nobody saw the moment he was resurrected. They found the sepulchre where Jesus was laid down, empty and made the conclusion that he was resurrected because the disciples and other witnesses saw him alive after the alleged crucifixion. Could it not be possible, as the Qur'an claims, that he didn't die on the cross?

C. Where is the proof then?

M. Let us see passages in the Bible supporting this evidence. Do you give more weight to what Jesus said or to hearsay of the disciples, apostles and other witnesses?

C. Of course more to Jesus himself.

M. That is in accordance with what Jesus said *(Matthew 10:24)*: "The disciple is not above his master, nor the servant above his lord."

C. But Jesus himself said that he will rise from the dead *(Luke 24:46)*: "And said unto them, Thus it is written, and thus it behoved Christ to suffer, and to rise from the dead the third day."

M. Suffering is often exaggerated in the Bible and termed "dead" as Paul said *(I Corinthians 15:31)*: "I protest by your rejoicing which I have in Christ, I die daily" (i.e. I suffer daily). Here are some of the proofs:

1. On the cross he beseeched God for help *(Matthew 27:46)*: "My God, my God, why hast thou forsaken me?" And in *Luke 22:42*, "Saying, Father if thou be willing, remove this cup from me; nevertheless not my will, but thine, be done." (This cup is the cup of death.)

2. Jesus' prayer not to die on the cross was accepted by God, according to Luke, Hebrews and James. Then how could he still die on the cross? *(Luke 22:43)*: "And there appeared an angel unto him from heaven, strengthening him." It means that an angel assured him that God would not leave him helpless *(Hebrews 5:7)*: "Who in the days of his flesh, when he [Jesus] had offered up prayers and supplications with strong crying and tears unto him that was able to save him from death, and was heard in that he feared."

    Jesus' prayers were here heard, which means answered in a positive way by God. *(James 5:16)*: "...The effectual fervent prayer of a righteous man availeth much." Jesus himself said *(Matthew 7:7-10)*: "Ask, and it shall be given you; seek, and ye shall find; knock, and it shall be opened unto you; For every one that asketh receiveth; and he that seeketh findeth, and to him who knocketh it shall be opened. Or what man is there of you, whom if his son ask bread, will he give him a stone? Or if he ask a fish, will he give him a serpent?" If all Jesus' prayers were accepted by God, including not to die on the cross, how could he still die on the cross then?

3. His legs were not broken by the Roman soldiers *(John 19:32-33)*: "Then came the soldiers, and brake the legs of the first, and of the other which was crucified with him. But when they

came to Jesus, and saw that he was dead already, they brake not his legs," Can you rely on these soldiers for pronouncing the death, or did they want to save Jesus as they found him innocent?

4. If Jesus died on the cross, his blood would clot and no blood would gush out of his body when his side was pierced. But the Gospel states that blood and water came out; *(John 19:34)*: "But one of the soldiers with a spear pierced his side, and forthwith came there out blood and water."

5. When the Pharises asked Jesus for a sign of his true mission he answered *(Matthew 12:40)*: "For as Jonas was three days and three nights in the whale's belly, so shall the Son of man be three days and three nights in the heart of the earth." Disregard now the time factor, which was also not three days and three nights but one day (Saturday, daytime only) and two nights (Friday night and Saturday night). Was Jonas alive in the belly of the whale?

C. Yes.

M. Was Jonas still alive when he was vomited out of the belly of the whale?

C. Yes.

M. Then Jesus was still alive as he prophesied.

6. Jesus himself stated that he didn't die on the cross. Early Sunday morning Mary Magdalene went to the sepulchre, which was empty. She saw somebody standing who looked like a gardener. She recognized him after conversation to be Jesus and wanted to touch him. Jesus said *(John 21:17)*: "Touch me not; for I am not yet ascended to my Father..." "Touch me not," perhaps because the

fresh wound would hurt him. "I am not yet ascended to my Father," means that he was still alive, not dead yet, because if somebody dies, then he goes back to the Creator. This was the strongest proof admitted by Jesus himself.

7. After the alleged crucifixion the disciples thought that he was not the same Jesus in body but spiritualized, because resurrected bodies are spiritualized.

C. Interruption. How could you be sure that resurrected bodies spiritualized?

M. That is what Jesus himself said in the Bible: that they are equal to angels.

C. Where in the Bible?

M. In *Luke 20:34-36*: "And answering said unto them, The children of the world marry, and are given in marriage. But they which shall be accounted worthy to obtain that world, and then resurrection from the dead, neither marry, nor are given in marriage: Neither can they die any more for they are equal unto the angels; and are the children of God, being the children of the resurrection."

Then Jesus convinced them by letting them touch his hands and feet, that he was the same person. As they could not believe him yet, he asked for meat to show them that he still are like any living individual. Read *Luke 24:36-41*, "And as they [the disciples] thus spake, Jesus himself stood in the midst of them, and saith unto them, Peace be unto you. But they were terrified and frightened, and supposed that they had seen a spirit. And he said unto them, Why are ye troubled? and why do thoughts arise in your hearts? Behold my hands and my feet, that it is I myself: handle me, and see; for a spirit hath not flesh and bones, as ye see me have. And when he had thus spoken, he shewed them his hands and his feet. And while they yet believed not for joy, and wondered, he said unto them, Have ye here any meat? And they gave him a piece of broiled fish, and of an honeycomb. And he took it, and did eat before them."

8. If you still believe that he died on the cross, then he was a false Prophet and accursed of God according to these passages: *(Deuteronomy 13:5)*: "And that Prophet, or that dreamer of dreams, shall be put to death..."; *(Deuteronomy 21:22-23)*: "And if a man have committed a sin worthy of death, and he be to be put to death, and thou hang him on a tree: His body shall not remain all night upon the tree, but thou shalt in any wise bury him that day; (for he that is hanged is accursed of God;) that thy land be not defiled, which the Lord thy God giveth thee for an inheritance."

To believe in his death on the cross is to discredit his prophethood. The Jews maintained to have killed Jesus on the cross and consequently portrayed him to be false in his claim to prophethood. Christians believe in the crucifixion necessary for their redemption of sin and consequently have to accept the accursedness of Jesus, too. This Christian belief opposes the Bible's teaching in *Hosea 6:6*, "For I desired mercy and not sacrifice; and the knowledge of God more than burnt-offerings." It also opposes Jesus' own teaching *(Matthew 9:13)*: "But go ye and learn what that meaneth, I will have mercy, and not sacrifice..." Again Jesus said *(Matthew 12:7)*: "But if ye had known what this meaneth, I will have mercy, and not sacrifice, ye would not have condemned the guiltless."

C. Why do people believe in the resurrection then?

M. It was Paul who taught the resurrection *(Acts 17:18)*: "...And some [Jews] said, What will this babbler say?

other some, He [Paul] seemeth to be a setter forth of strange gods: because he preached unto them Jesus, and the resurrection." Paul, who never saw Jesus, also admitted that the resurrection was his gospel *(II Timothy 2:8)*: "Remember that Jesus Christ of the seed of David was raised from the dead according to my gospel." He was also the first who declared Jesus as Son of God *(Acts 9:20)*: "And straightway he [Paul] preached Christ in the synagogues, that he is the Son of God." So Christianity is not a teaching of Jesus but of Paul.

C. But *Mark (16:19)* mentioned that Jesus was raised up to heaven and sat on the right hand of God: "So then after the Lord had spoken unto them, he was received up into heaven, and sat on the right hand of God."

M. As I told you under the discussion of the Holy Bible that *Mark 16, verses 9-20*, were expunged in certain Bibles. See remark in the Revised Standard Version, the New American Standard Bible and the New World Translation of the Holy Scriptures of the Jehovah's Witnesses Church. If you still believe that Jesus is divine because he was raised up to heaven, why don't you accept other Prophets as divine who were also raised up to heaven?

C. Who were they?

M. Elijah *(II Kings 2:11-12)*: "...and Elijah went up by a whirlwind into heaven. And Elisha saw it, and he cried...And he saw him no more..." Also Enoch was taken by God to heaven, "And Enoch walked with God; and he was not; for God took him." This was also repeated in *Hebrews 11:5*, "By faith Enoch was translated that he should not see death; and was not found, because God translated him; for before his translation he had this testimony, that he pleased God."

THE DOCTRINE OF ATONEMENT AND ORIGINAL SIN

C. So redemption of sin through the crucifixion is not Jesus' teaching?

M. This is the Doctrine of Atonement accepted by the Church three to four centuries after Jesus left the earth. It contradicts the Bible itself as the following passages show: *(Deuteronomy 24:16)*: "The fathers shall not be put to death for the children, neither shall the children be put to death for the father: every man shall be put to death for his own sin." *(Jeremiah 31:30)*: "But every one shall die for his own iniquity..." *(Ezekiel 18:20)*: "The soul that sinneth, it shall die. The son shall not bear the iniquity of the father, neither shall the father bear the iniquity of the son: the righteousness of the righteous shall be upon him, and the wickedness of the wicked shall be upon him." So Adam and Eve were responsible for their own sin, which had also been forgiven by Allah according to the Islamic version.

C. But these are in the Old Testament.

M. Read what Jesus himself said in *Matthew 7:1* and 2.

C. "Judge not, that ye be not judged. For with what judgment ye judge, ye shall be judged: and with what measure ye mete, it shall be measured to you again."

M. Read *I Corinthians 3:8*.

C. "Now he that planteth and he that watereth are one; and every man shall receive his own reward according to his own labour." But we believe in Original Sin!

M. Do you still want me to prove that children are born without sin? Read *Matthew 19:14*.

C. "But Jesus said, Suffer little children, and forbid them not, to come unto me: for of such is the kingdom of heaven."

M. So everybody is born without sin and all children belong to the kingdom of heaven. Do you know that it was Paul who abolished the Mosaic law? Read *Acts 13:39*.

C. "And by him all that believe are justified from all things, from which ye could not be justified by the law of Moses."

M. Let me ask a question. Why do you believe in the resurrection if Paul himself, who never saw Jesus alive, admitted that this was his gospel?

C. Where is it written?

M. Read *II Timothy 2:8*.

C. "Remember that Jesus Christ of the seed of David was raised from the dead according to my gospel." But why have we to believe that he was crucified and raised from the dead?

M. Yes, I do not know even. Islam is based on reason and is a pure teaching of all Prophets of Allah not contaminated with paganism and superstition.

C. That is what I am looking for.

M. Why don't you consider the Shahadah (Witness) or Testimony, first in English, then in Arabic. Let me help you pronounce it.

C. I bear witness that there is no deity but Allah Who has no partner and I bear witness that Muhammad is His slave servant and messenger. Ashhadu an la Ilaha illal-Lahu wahdahu la shareeka lahu, wa ash-hadu anna Muhammadan abduhu wa rasuluhu. Has Prophet Muhammad ﷺ then been prophesied in the Bible?

M. Yes, but it is not necessary for a Muslim to know it from the Bible. As you have studied the Bible I would like to discuss it with you briefly next time.

N.B. The rest of the discussion will be conducted between two Muslims: M and m.

MUHAMMAD ﷺ IN THE BIBLE

Both Ishmael and Isaac Were Blessed

M. Why did Ishmael and his mother Hagar leave Sarah?

m. After Isaac was weaned, his mother Sarah saw Ishmael mocking him, and didn't want Ishmael to be heir with her son Isaac *(Genesis 21:8-10)*: "And the child grew, and was weaned: and Abraham made a great feast the same day that Isaac was weaned. And Sarah saw the son of Hagar the Egyptian, which she had born unto Abraham, mocking. Wherefore she said unto Abraham, Cast out this bondwoman and her son: for the son of this bondwoman shall not be heir with my son, even with Isaac."

M. Isaac was about two years old when he was weaned. Ishmael was then sixteen years because Abraham was eighty-six years old when Hagar bore Ishmael and was a hundred years old when Isaac was born, according to *Genesis 16:16*, "And Abram was fourscore and six years old, when Hagar bare Ishmael to Abram," and *Genesis 21:5*, "And Abraham was a hundred years old, when his son Isaac was born unto him." *Genesis 21:8-10* is then in contradiction with *Genesis 21:14-21* where Ishmael was portrayed as a baby put on the shoulder of his mother, called lad and child, when both left Sarah: "And Abraham rose up early in the morning, and took bread. and a bottle of water, and gave it unto Hagar, putting it on her shoulder, and the child,... Arise, life up the lad, and hold him in thine hand..." This was the profile of a baby and not of a teenager. So Ishmael and his mother Hagar left Sarah long before Isaac was born. According to the Islamic version, Abraham took Ishmael and Hagar and made a new settlement in Mecca, called Paran in the Bible *(Genesis 21:21)*, because of a divine instruction given to Abraham as a part of God's plan. Hagar ran seven times between two hills, Safa and Marwa, looking for water; this became then an Islamic ritual for the annual pilgrimage in Mecca by millions of Muslims from all over the world. The well of water mentioned in *Genesis 21:19* is still present, now called Zamzam. Both Abraham and Ishmael later built the holy stone Ka'bah in Mecca. The spot where Abraham used to perform prayers near the Ka'bah is still present, now called Maqam Ibrahim, i.e. the Station of Abraham. During the days of pilgrimage, pilgrims in Mecca and Muslims all over the world commemorate the offering of Abraham and Ishmael by slaughtering cattle.

m. But the Bible mentions Isaac to be sacrificed.

M. No, the Islamic version states that the covenant between God, Abraham and his only son Ishmael was made and sealed when Ishmael was supposed to be sacrificed. And on the same day were Abraham, Ishmael and all men of the household circumcised while Isaac was not even born yet *(Genesis 17:24-27)* "And Abraham was ninety years old and nine, when he was circumcised in the flesh of his foreskin. And Ishmael his son was thirteen years old, when he was circumcised in the flesh of his foreskin. In the selfsame day was Abraham circumcised, and Ishmael his son. And all the men of his house, born in the house, and bought with money of the stranger, were circumcised with him."

A year later Isaac was born and circumcised when

he was eight days old *(Genesis 21:4-5)*: "And Abraham circumcised his son Isaac being eight days old, as God had commanded him. And Abraham was a hundred years old, when his son Isaac was born unto him."

So when the covenant was made and sealed (circumcision and sacrifice) Abraham was ninety-nine and Ishmael thirteen years old. Isaac was born a year later when Abraham was a hundred years old.

The descendants of Ishmael, Prophet Muhammad ﷺ, including all Muslims, remain faithful until today to this covenant of circumcision. In their prayers at least five times a day the Muslims include the praise of Abraham and his descendants with the praise of Muhammad ﷺ and his descendants.

m. But in *Genesis 22* it is mentioned that Isaac was to be sacrificed!

M. I know it, but you will see the contradiction there. It is mentioned there "thine only son Isaac." Should it not have been written "thine only son Ishmael" when Ismael was thirteen years old and Isaac not born yet? When Isaac was born Abraham had two sons. Because of chauvinism the name Ishmael was changed to Isaac in all of *Genesis 22*, but God had preserved the word "only" to show us what it should have been.

The words "I will multiply thy seed" in *Genesis 22:17* was applied earlier to Ishmael in *Genesis 16:10*. Was the whole of *Genesis 22* not applicable to Ishmael then? "I will make him a great nation" had been repeated twice for Ishmael in *Genesis 17:20* and *Genesis 21:18*, and never applied to Isaac at all.

m. The Jews and Christians maintain that Isaac was superior to Ishmael.

M. That is what they say but not what the Bible states *(Genesis 15:4)*: "And, behold, the word of the Lord came unto him [Abraham], saying, This [Eliezer of Damascus] shall not be thine heir, but he that shall come forth out of thine own bowels shall be thine heir." So Ishmael was also heir.

Genesis 16:10 "And the angel of the Lord said unto her [Hagar], I will multiply thy seed exceedingly, that it shall not be numbered for multitude."

Genesis 17:20, "And as for Ishmael, I have heard thee: Behold, I have blessed him, and will make him fruitful, and will multiply him exceedingly: twelve princes shall he beget, and I will make him a great nation."

Genesis 21:13, "And also of the son of the bondwoman will I make a nation, because he is thy seed."

Genesis 21:18, "Arise, lift up the lad [Ishmael], and hold him in thine hand for I will make him a great nation."

Deuteronomy 21:15-17, "If a man have two wives, one beloved, and another hated, and they have born him children, both the beloved and the hated; and if the firstborn son be hers that was hated: Then it shall be, when he maketh his sons to inherit that which he hath, that he may not make the son of the beloved firstborn before the son of the hated, which is indeed the firstborn: But he shall acknowledge the son of the hated for the firstborn, by giving him a double portion of all that he hath: for he is the beginning of the strength; the right of the firstborn is his." Islam does not deny God's blessings on Isaac and his descendants, but the son of promise is Ishmael from whom later arose Muhammad ﷺ as the Seal of all Prophets.

m. But Christians and Jews claim that Ishmael was an illegitimate son.

M. That is what they say, but not what the Bible states. How could a great Prophet like Abraham have an illegal wife and a son out of wedlock!

Genesis 16:3, "...and [Sarah] gave her [Hagar] to her husband Abram to be his wife." If the marriage was legal, how could their offspring be illegal then! Is a marriage between two foreigners, a Chaldean and an Egyptian, not more legal than a marriage between a man with a daughter of his father? Whether it was a lie of Abraham or not, it is stated in *Genesis 20:21*, "And yet indeed she [Sarah] is my sister; she is the daughter of my father, but not the daughter of my mother; and she became my wife."

The name Ishmael was also chosen by Allah Himself *(Genesis 16:11)*: "And the Angel of the Lord said unto her [Hagar], Behold, thou art with child, and shalt bear a son, and shalt call his name Ishmael, because the Lord hath heard thy affliction." Ishmael means God Hears. And where in the Bible is it written that Ishmael was an illegitimate son?

m. Nowhere in the Bible.

M. Long before both Ishmael and Isaac were born, Allah made a covenant with Abraham *(Genesis 15:18)*: "...saying, Unto thy seed have I given this land, from the river of Egypt unto the great river, the Euphrates." Was not the greater part of Arabia lying between the Nile and the Euphrates, where later all the descendants of Ishmael were settling?

m. Do you mean that no land was promised to Isaac and his descendants?

M. We Muslims never deny that Isaac was also blessed. See *Genesis 17:8*, "And I will give unto thee, and to thy seed [Isaac] after thee, the land wherein thou art a stranger, all the land Canaan, for an everlasting possession; and I will be their God."

Do you also see the difference that Abraham was mentioned "a stranger" in Canaan but not in the land between the Nile and the Euphrates. As a Chaldean he was more an Arab than a Jew.

m. But the Covenant was made with Isaac according to *Genesis 17:21*, "But my covenant will I establish with Isaac, which Sarah shall bear unto thee at this time in the next year,"

M. Does this exclude Ishmael? Where in the Bible does it say that Allah would not make any covenant with Ishmael?

m. Nowhere.

Criterion of the Prophet by Jeremiah

Jeremiah 28:9, "The Prophet which prophesieth of peace, when the word of the Prophet shall come to pass, then shall the prophet be known, that the Lord hath truly sent him."

The word Islam also signifies Tranquillity, Peace. Peace between the Creator and his creatures. This prophecy of Jeremiah cannot be applied to Jesus, as he himself stated that he didn't come for peace *(Luke 12:51-53)*: "Suppose ye that I am come to give peace on earth? I tell you, Nay; but rather division: For from henceforth there will be five in one house divided, three against two and two against three. The father shall be divided against the son, and the son against the father; the mother against the daughter, and the daughter against the mother; the mother inlaw against her daughter inlaw, and the daughter inlaw against her mother inlaw." See also *Matthew 10:34-36*.

Until Shiloh Come

This was a message of Jacob to his children before he

died. *(Genesis 49:1)*: "And Jacob called unto his sons, and said, Gather yourselves together, that I may tell you that which shall befall you in the last days."

Genesis 49:10, "The sceptre shall not depart from Judah, nor a lawgiver from between his feet, until Shiloh come; and unto him shall the gathering of the people be."

Shiloh is also the name of a town but its real meaning is peace, tranquillity, rest, i.e., Islam. It could never refer to a town here. If it referred to a person, it could be a corruption of Shaluah (Elohim), i.e. Messenger (of Allah).

So the Israelite Prophethood in the lineage of Isaac would stop as soon as Shiloh comes. This corresponds with *Surah 2:133*, "Were you witnesses when death came to Jacob? When he said to his sons, "What will you worship after me?" They said, "We shall worship your God [Allah], the God of your fathers Abraham, Ishmael and Isaac, One God and to Him we surrender [in Islam]."

The shift of Prophethood to another nation was threatened in *Jeremiah 31:36*, "If those ordinances depart from before me, saith the Lord, then the seed of Israel also shall cease from being a nation before me for ever." Also hinted by Jesus in *Matthew 21:43*, "Therefore say I unto you, The kingdom of God shall be taken from you, and given to a nation bringing forth the fruits thereof."

Baca Is Mecca

The Holy Ka'bah built by Abraham and his son Ishmael is in Mecca. This name Mecca (Makkah) has been mentioned one time in the Holy Qur'an is *Surah 48:24*. Another name for Mecca is Bakka, depending on the dialect of the tribe. This also has been mentioned one time, in *Surah 3:96*, "Verily, the first House [of worship] appointed for mankind was that in Bakka [Mecca], full of blessing, and guidance for all people." Amazing enough, this word Bakka was mentioned by Prophet David in his *Psalms 84:6*: "Who passing through the valley of Baca make it a well, the rain also filleth the pools." The well here is the well-known well of Zamzam, still present now, close to the Ka'bah.

The House of My Glory

Isaiah, *chapter 60*:

1. "Arise, shine; for thy light is come, and the glory of the Lord is risen upon thee." Compare with *Surah 74:1-3*, "O, you [Muhammad ﷺ], wrapped up in garments! Arise and warn! And your Lord magnify!"

2. "For, behold, the darkness shall cover the earth, and gross darkness the people: but the Lord shall arise upon thee, and his glory shall be seen upon thee." The advent of Prophet Muhammad ﷺ was at a time of darkness when the world forgot the Oneness of God as taught by Abraham and all other Prophets including Jesus.

3. "And the Gentiles shall come to thy light, and kings to the brightness of thy rising."

4. "Lift up thine eyes round about, and see: all they gather themselves together, they come to thee:..." Within less than twenty-three years the whole of Arabia was united.

5. "...because the abundance of the sea shall be converted unto thee, the forces of the Gentiles shall come unto thee." Within less than a century Islam spread out of Arabia to other countries.

6. "The multitude of camels shall cover thee, the dromedaries of Midian and Ephah; all they from Sheba shall come, they shall bring gold and incense; and they shall shew forth the praises of the Lord."

7. "All the flocks Kedar shall be gathered together unto

thee, the rams of Nebaioth shall minister unto thee; they shall come up with acceptance on mine altar, and I will glorify the house of my glory." The tribes of Kedar (Arabia) who were divided were then united. "The house of my glory" referred here to the House of Allah in Mecca and not the Church of Christ as thought by Christian commentators. It is a fact that the villages of Kedar (now whole Saudi Arabia at least) are the only country of the world which remains impenetrable to any influence of the Church.

11. "Therefore thy gates shall be open continually: they shall not be shut day not night; that men may bring unto thee the forces of the Gentiles, and that their kings may be brought." It is a fact that the mosque surrounding the Holy Ka'bah in Mecca has remained open day and night since it was cleansed by Prophet Muhammad ﷺ from the idols 1400 years ago. Rulers as well as subjects came for Pilgrimage.

Chariot of Asses and Chariot of Camels

The vision of Isaiah of the two riders in *Isaiah 21:7*, "And he saw a chariot with a couple of horsemen, a chariot of asses, and a chariot of camels;..."

Who was the rider upon an ass? Every Sunday School student will know him. That was Jesus *(John 12:14)*: "And Jesus, when he had found a young ass, sat thereon; as it is written."

Who, then, is the promised rider on a camel? This powerful Prophet has been overlooked by Bible readers. This is Prophet Muhammad ﷺ. If this is not applied to him, then the prophecy has yet to be fulfilled. That is why Isaiah mentioned further in the same *chapter (21:13)*: "The burden upon Arabia..." which means the responsibility of the Arab Muslims, and of course now of all Muslims, to spread the message of Islam.

Isaiah 21:14, "The inhabitants of the land of Tema

brought water to him that was thirsty, they prevented with their bread him that fled." Tema is probably Madina where Prophet Muhammad ﷺ and his companions immigrated to. Each immigrant was brothered by one inhabitant of Madina and given food and shelter.

Isaiah 21:15, "For they fled from the swords, from the drawn sword and from the bent bow, and from the grievousness of war." This was when Prophet Muhammad ﷺ and his companions were persecuted and left Mecca for Madina.

Isaiah 21:16, "For thus hath the Lord said unto me, Within a year, according to the years of an hireling, and all the glory of Kedar shall fail." Exactly in the second year of Hijrah (immigration) the pagans were defeated in the battle of Badr.

Finally *Isaiah 21:17* concludes with "...the mighty men of the children of Kedar, shall be diminished: for the Lord God of Israel hath spoken it." Kedar is the second son of Ishmael *(Genesis 25:13)* from whom ultimately Prophet Muhammad ﷺ arose. In the beginning the children of Kedar were attacking Muhammad ﷺ and his companions. But as many of them accepted Islam, the number of children of Kedar who resisted, diminished. In some Bible verses Kedar is synonymous with Arab in general, as in *Ezekiel 27:21*, "Arabia, and all the Princes of Kedar..."

The Prophet Like Unto Moses

God addressed Moses *(Deuteronomy 18:18)*: "I will raise them up a Prophet from among their brethren, like unto thee [Moses], and will put my words in his mouth; and he shall speak unto them all that I shall command him."

1. Brethren of Israelites (descendants of Abraham

through Isaac) are Ishmaelites (descendants of Abraham through Ishmael). Jesus is here excluded as he is an Israelite; otherwise it should be written "a Prophet from among yourselves."

2. Is Muhammad ﷺ not like unto Moses? If not accepted, this promise has yet to be fulfilled. The table below, taken from *Al-Ittihad, January-March 1982, page 41*, is self-explanatory:

Following is a comparison between a few crucial characteristics of Moses, Muhammad and Jesus which may clarify the identify of "that prophet" who was to come after Moses:

Area of Comparison	Moses	Muhammad	Jesus
Birth	Usual	Usual	Unusual
Family life	Married, children	Married, children	No marriage or children
Death	Usual	Usual	Unusual
Career	Prophet/Statesman	Prophet/Statesman	Prophet
Forced Emigration (in adulthood)	To Median	To Madinah	None
Encounter with enemies	Hot pursuit	Hot Pursuit/Battles	No-similar encounter
Results of encounter	Moral/Physical Victory	Moral/Physical Victory	Moral Victory
Writing down of revelation	In his lifetime (Torah)	In his lifetime (Al-Qur'an)	After him
Nature of teachings	Spiritual/legal	Spiritual/legal	Mainly spiritual
Acceptance of leadership (by his people)	Rejected, then accepted	Rejected, then accepted	Rejected (by most Israelites)

3. "put my words in his mouth." So God's revelation came through Gabriel, and Prophet Muhammad's ﷺ own thinking was not involved. But this applied to all Divine revelation. Perhaps here mentioned specifically because compared with the revelation to Moses which came in "written tablets" as believed.

Deuteronomy 18:19, "And it shall come to pass that whosoever will not hearken unto my words which he shall speak in my name, I will require it of him."

In the *Qur'an* 113 of the 114 *chapters* (Surah) start with "In the name of Allah, most Gracious, most Merciful." Also, in their daily work the Muslims start with this saying. Not in the name of God, but "in my name," His Personal name which is "Allah." As it is a personal name, it is not subject to gender like God or Goddess, or to plurality like God or Gods. Christians start with "In the name of the Father, the Son and the Holy Spirit."

It is to be noted that those who will not hear him, or who deny him, will be punished. This corresponds with passages in the Holy Qur'an: *(Surah 3:19)*: "Truly the religion in the sight of Allah is Islam." *(Surah 3:85)*: "And whoever desires a religion other than Islam, it will never be accepted of him, and in the Hereafter he will be one of the losers."

My Servant, Messenger and Elect

A clearer fulfillment of the prophecy of Muhammad ﷺ is found is *Isaiah 42*:

1. "Behold my servant, whom I uphold; mine elect, in whom my soul delighteth; I have put my spirit upon him: he shall bring forth judgment to the Gentiles." Also called "my messenger" in *verse 19*. No doubt all Prophets were indeed servants, messengers and elect of Allah. Yet no Prophet is universally called by these specific titles as Muhammad ﷺ in Arabic "Abduhu wa Rasuluhul Mustafa," i.e. His slave servant and His elected messenger. The testimony of a person accepting Islam is: "I bear witness that there is no deity but Allah Who has no partner and I bear witness that Muhammad ﷺ is His servant and messenger." This same formula is repeated five

times a day through the minarets as a call for prayers, another five times daily, immediately before the beginning of each prayer, nine times a day in the Tashahhud during the minimum obligatory prayers, several more times if a Muslim performs additional recommended prayers. The most common title of Prophet Muhammad ﷺ is Rasoolullah, i.e. the messenger of Allah.

2. "He shall not cry, not lift up, nor cause his voice to be heard in the street." This describes the decency of Prophet Muhammad ﷺ.

3. "...he shall bring forth judgment unto truth."

4. "He shall not fail nor be discouraged, till he have set judgment in the earth: and the isles shall wait for his law." This is to be compared with Jesus, who did not prevail over his enemies and was disappointed because of the rejection by the Israelites.

5. ...

6. "I the Lord have called thee in righteousness, and will hold thine hand, and will keep thee, and give thee for a covenant of the people, for a light of the Gentiles." "and will keep thee," i.e. no other Prophet will come after him. In a short time many Gentiles were guided into Islam.

7. "To open the blind eyes, to bring out the prisoners from the prison, and them that sit in darkness out of the prison house." "Blind eyes, life of darkness" denotes here the pagan life. "Bring out the prisoners from the prison" denotes the abolishment of slavery for the first time in the history of mankind.

8. "I am the Lord: that is my name: and my glory will I not give to another, neither my praise to graven images." Prophet Muhammad ﷺ is unique among all Prophets as he is the "Seal of all Prophets" and

his teachings remain undistorted until today, compared with Christianity and Judaism.

9. ...

10. "Sing unto the Lord a new song, and his praise from the end of the earth,...." A new song as it is not in Hebrew or Aramaic, but in Arabic. The praise of God and His messenger Muhammad ﷺ is chanted five times daily from the minarets of millions of mosques all over the world.

11. "Let the wilderness and the cities thereof lift up their voice, the villages that Kedar doth inhabit: let the inhabitants of the rock sing, let them shout from the top of the mountains." From Mount Arafat near Mecca the Pilgrims chant every year the following: "Here I come [for Your service] O, Allah. Here I come. Here I come. There is no partner with you. Here I come. Verily Yours is the praise, the blessings and sovereignty. There is no partner besides You." *Isaiah 42* can never be applied to an Israelite Prophet as Kedar is the second son of Ishmael. See *Genesis 25:13*.

12. "Let them give glory unto the Lord, and declare his praise in the islands." And really Islam spread to the small islands as far as Indonesia and the Caribbean Sea.

13. "...he shall prevail against his enemies." In a short period the Kingdom of God on earth was established with the advent of Muhammad ﷺ, this 42nd chapter of Isaiah fits exactly to the character of Prophet Muhammad ﷺ.

King David Called Him "My Lord"

Psalms 110:1, "The Lord said unto my Lord, Sit thou at my right hand, until I make thine enemies thy footstool."

There were mentioned here two Lords. If the first

Lord (the speaker) is God, the second Lord (the one spoken to) could not be God also, as David knew only One God. So it should read: "God said unto my Lord,..." Who was that whom David called "my Lord"? The Church would say Jesus. But this had been denied by Jesus himself in *Matthew 22:45, Mark 12:37* and *Luke 20:44*. He excluded himself from this title as he was a son of David. How could David call him "my Lord" if he was his son, he argued. Jesus said *(Luke 20:42-44)*: "How say they that Christ is David's son? And David himself saith in the book of Psalms, The Lord said unto my Lord, Sit thou on my right hand, Till I make thine enemies thy footstool. David therefore calleth him Lord, how is he then his son?"

Jesus must have given answer not recorded in the four canonical Gospels, but mentioned explicitly in the Gospel of Barnabas that the promise was made in Ishmael, not in Isaac. David's Lord was thus Muhammad ﷺ whom he saw in spirit. No Prophet ever accomplished more than Muhammad ﷺ. Even the work of all other Prophets together is still small compared with what Muhammad ﷺ did within a short period of 23 years, and which remains unchanged until now.

Art Thou That Prophet?

The Jews sent priests and Levites to John the Baptist to inquire who he really was. *(John 1:20-21)*: "And he [John the Baptist] confessed and denied not; but confessed, I am not the Christ. And they asked him, What then? Art thou Elias? And he saith, I am not. Art thou that prophet? And he answered, No."

The crucial question here is: Art thou that Prophet? Who was then the long-awaited Prophet after the advent of Jesus and John the Baptist? Was he not the one like unto Moses *(Deuteronomy 18:18)* who is Muhammad ﷺ?

Baptizing with the Holy Ghost and with Fire

Matthew 3:11: "I [John the Baptist] indeed baptize you with water unto repentance: but he that cometh after me is mightier than I, whose shoes I am not worthy to bear: he shall baptize you with the Holy Ghost, and with fire."

If Jesus was alluded to here, John the Baptist would not go back to live in the jungle again, but to cling to him and be one of his disciples, which he did not do. So another powerful Prophet was here alluded to, and not Jesus. The one coming after John the Baptist could not be Jesus as both were contemporaries. Here again, was it not Prophet Muhammad ﷺ alluded to by John the Baptist?

The Least in the Kingdom of Heaven

Jesus was quoted as saying (Matthew 11:11): "Verily I say unto you, Among them that are born of women there hath not risen a greater than John the Baptist: notwithstanding he that is least in the kingdom of heaven is greater than he."

Can you believe that John the Baptist is greater than Adam, Noah, Abraham, Moses, David and many other Prophets? How many pagans had John the Baptist converted and how many followers did he have? But this is not the main point here. The question is: who was the least in the kingdom of heaven, greater than John the Baptist? For sure not Jesus, as at that time the kingdom of heaven was not yet formed, and he never claimed to be the least, i.e. the youngest one. The kingdom of heaven consists of God as the Supreme Being and all prophets. The least or youngest one is here Prophet Muhammad ﷺ.

Blessed Are the Peacemakers

In his sermon on the mount Jesus was quoted as saying (Matthew 5:9): "Blessed are the peacemakers: for they shall be called the children of God."

Islam means also Peace: peace between the Creator and the worshiper. Jesus could not mean his mission as peacemaker as he did not come for peace. *(Matthew 10:34-36)*: "Think not that I am come to send peace on earth: I came not to send peace, but a sword. For I am come to set a man at variance against his father, and the daughter against her mother, and the daughter-in-law against her mother-in-law. And a man's foes shall be they of his own household." See also *Luke 12:49-53*.

Comforter

John 14:16, "And I will pray the Father, and he shall give you another Comforter, that he may abide with you for ever."

We do not know exactly the original Aramaic word used by Jesus for Comforter. Other Bibles use Consoler, Advocate, Helper, and in Greek Bibles the word Paraclete. There are different explanations for it: Holy Spirit, the Word, a person, etc.

The Holy Qur'an states in *Surah 61:6* that Jesus explicitly mentioned the name Ahmad: "And (remember) when Jesus Son of Mary said: "O, children of Israel! I am the Apostle of Allah (sent) to you comfirming the Torah (which came) before me, and giving glad tidings of an Apostle to come after me, whose name shall be Ahmad (i.e. the second name of Prophet Muhammad , and literally it means the one who praises Allah more than others)."

Whatever the explanation is of the Comforter, we conclude that Jesus left an unfinished work and that someone was coming to complete his mission. Let us examine in the light of the Bible if this Comforter fits the character of Prophet Muhammad :

1. "another Comforter": So many Comforters had come and another one was to come.

2. "that he may abide with you for ever": as there was no need for another one to come after him, and he was the Seal of all Prophets. The teaching will abide for ever, will remain intact. In fact the Holy Qur'an and all his teaching remain as they were 1400 years ago.

3. "he will reprove the world of sin" *(John 16:8)*: all other Prophets, even Abraham, Moses, David and Solomon chastised their neighbor's and their people for sin, but not the world as Muhammad ﷺ did. He not only rooted out idolatry in Arabia within a 23-year period, but also sent envoys to Heraclius, the Sovereigns of the empires of Persia and Rome, to Najashi, the King of Ethiopia and to Muqauqis, the Governor of Egypt.

   He reprimanded the Christians for dividing the Unity of God into trinity, for having raised Jesus to Son of God and God Himself. It was he who condemned the Jews and Christians for having corrupted their Scriptures, demonstrated the birthright of Ishmael, and cleared the Prophets from accusations of adultery, incest, rape and idolatry.

4. "the prince of the world is judged" *(John 16:11)*. This is Satan as explained in *John 12:31* and *14:30*. So Prophet Muhammad ﷺ come to chastise the world on account of judgement.

5. "the Spirit of Truth" *(John 16:13)*. Since childhood Prophet Muhammad ﷺ was called Al-Ameen, i.e. the Honest or Truthful One, and "he will guide you into all truth:..." *(John 16:13)*.

6. "For he shall not speak of himself, but whatsoever he shall hear, that shall he speak" *(John 16:13)*.

   The Holy Qur'an is God's word. Not a single word from Prophet Muhammad ﷺ or his companion was included. The angel Gabriel read it to him, he memorized it and it was written down by his scribes. His own sayings and teachings were recorded in Hadith or Tradition (plural, Ahadith).

Compare with *Deuteronomy 18:18*, "...and will put my words in his mouth; and he shall speak unto them all that I shall command him." This corresponds with *Surah 53:2-4*: "Your companion [Muhammad] is neither astray nor being misled. Nor does he speak of [his own] desire. It is only the inspiration that is inspired."

7. "and he will shew you things to come" *(John 16:13)*. All prophecies of Prophet Muhammad came to pass.

8. "He shall glorify me" *(John 16:14)*. Actually the Holy Qur'an and Prophet Muhammad ﷺ have more reverence for Jesus ﷺ than the Bible and Christians themselves. The following will clarify:

   a. to believe in his death on the cross discredits his prophethood according to *Deuteronomy 13:5*, "And that prophet, or that dreamer of dreams, shall be put to death..." It also stamps him as accursed (May Allah forbid!) according to *Deuteronomy 21:22-23*: "...for he that is hanged is accursed of God..."

   b. *Matthew 27:46*, "...My God, my God, why hast thou forsaken me?" Could this not come from someone other than Jesus? Even a non-prophet would smile at agony as he knew that his death would win him the title of martyr. Was this not an insult of Jesus in not having faith in Allah?

   c. We Muslims cannot believe that Jesus could label the Gentiles as dogs and swine and address his mother with Woman, as the Holy Qur'an states in *Surah 19:32*, "And dutiful to my Mother [i.e. Mary], and [Allah] made me not an unblessed and arrogant." *Matthew 7:6*, "Give not that which is holy unto the dogs, neither cast ye your pearls before swine..." *John*

2:4, "Jesus saith unto her [Mary], Woman, what have I to do with thee?"

Revelation to Prophet Muhammad ﷺ

The first revelation of Allah through the angel Gabriel to Muhammad ﷺ was the word "Iqra" which means "Read" in *Surah 96:1-5*. As he was illiterate, he replied: "I cannot read." This first revelation was prophesied in *Isaiah 29:12*, "And the book is delivered to him that is not learned, saying, Read this, I pray thee and he saith, I am not learned."

The order of the revelations is not as the order it is seen in the Qur'an. In other words the first part revealed is not in the first page and the last part revealed is not in the last page. That these revelations came in instalments and inserted in certain order in the Qur'an as ordained by Allah, was also mentioned in *Isaiah 28:10-11*, "For precept must be upon precept, precept upon precept; line upon line, here a little, and there a little: For with stammering lips and another tongue will he speak to his people." Another tongue means here another language, not Hebrew or Aramaic but Arabic.

Muslims all over the world are using one language, which is Arabic, in calling their God, in their prayers, pilgrimage and in their greetings to each other. Also this unity of language had been prophesied in *Zephaniah 3:9*, "For then will I turn to the people a pure language, that they may all call upon the name of the Lord, to serve him with one consent." Alas the Truth has come in Arabic, but some still expect Prophet Jesus, who might teach mankind to worship Allah in one unique language in his second coming will join the Muslim in their mosques as he is like any other Muslim, circumcised, not eating pork, and performing prayers with ablution, standing, bowing and prostration.

REFERENCES

1. Explanatory English Translation of Holy Qur'an, by Dr. Muhammad Taqui-Din Al-Hilali and Dr. Muhammad Muhsin Khan.
2. The Holy Bible, King James Version, authorized 1611.
3. The Holy Bible, Revised Standard Version.
4. New World Translation of the Holy Scriptures: Jehovah's Witnesses Church.
5. New American Standard Bible.
6. The Myth of the Cross, by A.D. Ajijola.
7. The Cross and the Crescent, by Maulana Muhammad Imran.
8. Davis Dictionary of the Bible, 1980.
9. The International Standard Bible Encyclopedia.
10. Smith's Bible Dictionary, 1980.
11. Encyclopedia Britannica, 1980.
12. Muhammad in the Bible, by Prof. Abdul-Ahad Dawud.
13. Muhammad in the Bible, by Ahmed Deedat.
14. Jesus, A Prophet of Islam, by Sulaiman Shahid Mufassir.
15. Biblical Studies from Muslim Perspectives, by S. Mufassir.
16. Muhammad in the Bible, by Jamal Badawi: *Al-Ittihad*, January-March, 1982.